Mountain bikes maintenance and repair

Mountain Bikes Maintenance and Repair

John Stevenson and Brant Richards

Bicycle Books, Inc.

Published by: Bicycle Books, Inc, P O Box 2038, Mill Valley, CA 94942 Tel.: (415) 381 2515

Distributed to the book trade by: (USA) National Book Network, Lanham, MD
(Canada) Raincoast Book Distribution Ltd., Vancouver, BC

Library of Congress Cataloging in Publication Data

Stevenson, John, and Brant Richards.
Mountain Bikes: Maintenance and Repair.
Second revised, expanded and updated edition.
Bibliography: p. includes index.
1. Bicycles and bicycling – manuals, handbooks, etc.
2. Authorship – manuals, handbooks etc.
I. Title.
Library of Congress Catalog Card Number
93-72508
ISBN 0-933201-60-5 Paperback original

First edition 1992
Second edition 1994

Acknowledgements:
The authors and publishers would like to thank: Lesleigh and Jill; Chris and Tym; Morph DT
and all at Stif; Karen at Madison; Nick at Trek; Chipps; Lloyd at ID; Peter at Superspray; the
MBUK crew; Adrian and Duncan; Ian at Berkshire Cycles; James Tatlow; Michael Bonney;
Curly the Cop at Pedal Power; all at Pedro's Lube; and Les at Stuart Bikes. Grateful thanks
are also extended to Steve Behr of Stockfile for supplying all of the photography.

Design: Chris Hand, Design for Print
Typesetting: Paragon Typesetters, Queensferry, Clwyd
Printed and bound in England by the Alden Press, Oxford

Contents

1: INTRODUCTION

The mountain bike has been one of the phenomena of recent years. Its durability, practicality and comfort have brought millions of people to cycling who would never have considered riding a bike, on or off road; and the resulting boom in world bike sales has funded a significant improvement in the quality and performance of the equipment that is available to all types of cyclist. Whether you race, commute, tour or just ride a mountain bike for the sheer joy of getting out into the countryside, this manual is intended to help you get more out of your mountain bike by keeping it in the best possible mechanical condition.

At its heart, the mountain bike is still a machine and like any machine it needs a certain amount of regular attention to keep it working at its best. Regularly maintaining your mountain bike has lots of benefits besides just keeping it working properly. First of all, of course, there's the financial factor: a good

mechanic charges a good hourly rate, and although good mechanics are fast (that's one of the things that makes them good mechanics) it's still cheaper to maintain your own bike, provided you can spare the evening that any routine job will take.

The other half of the financial equation is that a well-maintained bike costs less to run in the long term. Worn bike parts cause secondary wear to other components if you don't replace them promptly. A classic example of this is the chain, which will wear out the sprockets and chainrings to the point where a new chain will not work with them. If the chain is replaced before it is too worn, the sprockets and rings last much longer. Secondly, there's the certainty of knowing that your bike is working right because you checked it over last.

During his brief and unstartling racing career John turned up for an event with a bike that had just had a new rear wheel fitted, and our colleague at the bike shop we used to work in had put the tyre back on and pumped it up harder than John was used to. He forgot to check the tyre pressure before he got to the start line and spent the first lap of the race getting bounced around by the over-hard tyre until he finally stopped to let out a few psi. If he'd inflated it himself he'd have had no such problem.

1988 World Champion Mike Kloser takes this attitude to its logical extreme, and can frequently be seen stripping and reassembling his bike in the hotel, the evening before a race, until he is completely happy that it is working perfectly. Lining up at the start and being absolutely certain that your bike works perfectly leaves your mind clear to concentrate on racing. As Mike puts it, 'You don't want to be there on the start line wondering whether your bike's gonna make it.' Thirdly, knowing how your bike works and how to fix it is extremely useful if it breaks down while you're out on the trails. A minor mechanical problem can become a major disaster if you're miles from nowhere with no tools. Riders who carry a basic tool kit and know how to use it will also find they get invited on more rides!

Lastly, working on your bike is intrinsically satisfying. Learning how to use the tools of the bike mechanic's trade is an enjoyable process and the end result, a fund of knowledge that allows you to bail your friends out of mechanical troubles that they consider insoluble, is extremely useful and can be lucrative; most professional mechanics are self-taught. John once had to service a badly jammed Shimano hub, the result of misadjustment by a so-called mechanic who didn't know what he was doing. When he started the part looked like a write-off, and the owner was contemplating buying a new hub and having the wheel rebuilt. Stripping the thing down proved

difficult, but once it was apart the fault was actually quite simple and easy to cure. The really enjoyable part of this job was not the mere fact of helping out a friend, but the satisfaction of resurrecting an apparently terminally ill component.

Despite these advantages most people seem afraid to tackle even the most basic jobs on their bikes. We've seen bikes checked into dealer's workshops for the most minor problems: maladjusted gears, misaligned stems, punctures. There is a myth that bike mechanics have some sort of mystical 'mechanical aptitude' which gives them a supernatural rapport with the cold steel and aluminium of modern mountain bikes. While a few such individuals undoubtedly exist (they are called wheel-builders, and we will look at their skills in a later chapter) anyone can pick up the necessary mechanical skills to do most of the routine jobs on a mountain bike, given the right tools and a little time and practice.

John was utterly ham-fisted in 'technical' subjects at school and still runs a mile when presented with a wood plane or a precision filing job but can tweak bike components as well as anyone, though usually not as quickly as some. Brant, on the other hand, has a combination of a raging desire to tinker with things and a mechanical engineering degree that, to the uninitiated, might look like 'mechanical aptitude'.

In reality, it's all down to practise and familiarity with the equipment. We didn't actually start doing our own maintenance until our late teens. The biking bug was beginning to bite deep and we were impecunious students. We learned from necessity because if we didn't do our own repairs we couldn't afford to ride. Within a couple of years we were working as part-time mechanics in a bike shop. Nevertheless we're not 'natural' mechanics. We didn't dismantle our dad's cars when we were 12, then reassemble it so it worked perfectly and then make a profit on the two boxes of parts we had left over, or build model aeroplanes that covered ridiculous distances, and you don't need to have either. Anyone can learn how to fix bikes. Anyone.

The vital things are tools and time. We'll look at tool kits later, but the other half of that pairing is time. We know people who can quite cheerfully stand with a brazing torch in hand putting the final touches to the frame that they are going touring on next day, but this is not a sensible attitude for a rookie mechanic to take. Give yourself plenty of time for any job, preferably an open-ended amount of it. Nothing is worse than attempting to adjust a hub 15 minutes before you're going riding; every attempt at haste will just make you more clumsy. Do it the day before, preferably while there's a bike shop open so that you can get help if you get irretrievably stuck.

Another myth about the ability to repair and maintain bikes is that it's a secondary sexual characteristic, that the only people who can possibly be good mechanics are men, because the ability to wield a spanner is somehow passed from generation to generation on the Y chromosome. This is clearly nonsense, and it's encouraging to see that the number of female pro mechanics has grown dramatically over the last few years.

One of the owners at the bike shop we used to work at was a woman in her mid-twenties called Rachel. Like us, Rachel started learning mechanics while she was at college. 'I started fixing my own bike after watching other people fix it for me, and realising it really wasn't that difficult. Once you've seen things done, you realise that they're quite easy and then it's just a matter of having the right tools and the confidence to tackle things yourself. 'Rachel learned by watching other riders, and by hanging out at her local bike shop. You can learn a lot by being a bike shop hanger on, and she had the good luck to be able to ask someone if she got into problems. This is a common way to learn — most mechanics are happy to tell you how to do things (as long as they're not too busy) — it gives them a chance to display the knowledge that they've accumulated over the years.

Rachel teaches a bike maintenance class for women and comments that the commonest problem she encounters among her pupils is simple ignorance about the innards of bike components. From the outside, a bottom bracket bearing can be a complete mystery, but as she says 'once you get it apart, and see that it's just a cup and a cone — there's nothing you can break, and you can just take your time and fiddle with it until it's right — then you get more confident.' She adds a crucial point about maintenance: 'I've taught a lot of people how to recognise faults. I think most people would be able to do a job, but they don't realise they've got a problem until it's too late. You've got to learn that a particular rattle can mean that your headset is loose. This book will, we hope, help you learn what a particular rattle means, and how you should fix it.

The first edition of *Mountain Bikes: Maintenance and Repair* was successful beyond our most optimistic expectations, and we'd like to kick off by thanking everyone who said how much they enjoyed it, and found it useful. Your encouragement was an inspiration when the time came to sit down and compile this revised and (we hope) improved edition. We'd also like to thank everyone who has pointed out mistakes, and unclear instructions, in the first edition; your constructive criticism has helped us to fine-tune this version.

Who is this book for? One of the criticisms that was occasionally levelled at us was that we didn't go into enough detail about some jobs. The very good reason for this was, and still is, that this book is not aimed at the professional or semi-professional mechanic, but at the relative beginner who perhaps still finds the in-your-face expertise of some bike shops a bit daunting. Aspiring pro mechanics should equip themselves with Barnett's Manual and Sutherland's Handbook, which together form a thick and expensive library for the pro mechanic, though we hope they will find a few new ideas, and some entertainment, in this book.

2: TOOLS OF THE TRADE

It's a truism that the bad workman blames his or her tools, but the flipside of this cliché is that nobody can do a good job without reasonably good quality tools. This doesn't mean that the rookie mechanic should rush out and spend hundreds of pounds on a full set of Park or Campagnolo tools, just that if you are going to make an investment in a tool kit it's worth buying good quality.

Tools fall into two categories: normal tools, which you can get from any good hardware shop and which includes spanners, Allen keys, screwdrivers and pliers; and specialist tools, which are unique to bikes and can be had from well-stocked dealers.

The extent and quality of the tools you buy will depend on the level of repairs you want to attempt, and generally tool kits can be grouped into five classes: basic, intermediate, advanced, professional and trail.

The basic tool kit

A basic tool kit contains what you need to adjust and maintain all parts of the bike except the bearings and wheels. With basic tools you will be able to adjust gears and brakes and replace the expendable parts of these systems — that is the cables, brake blocks and gear jockey wheels — and the components themselves. Basic tools also allow you to adjust or replace the handlebar and stem, the saddle, and of course the tyres and inner tubes.

This is all many riders will need. Jobs like dismantling and regreasing the bearings of the hubs, headset and bottom bracket need doing infrequently and can be left to a bike shop. The basic tool kit is the minimum you'll need to work efficiently and effectively on your bike, and usually contains the following:

- **Combination spanners: 8mm, 9mm, 10mm**
- **Socket spanners: 8mm, 9mm, 10mm**
- **Allen keys: 2mm, 2.5mm, 3mm, 4mm, 5mm, 6mm, 8mm, 10mm**
- **Combination pliers**
- **Cable cutters**
- **Small cross-head screwdriver**
- **Small flat-blade screwdriver**
- **Large flat-blade screwdriver**
- **8inch adjustable spanner**
- **Cable puller (optional)**
- **Chain cleaner**
- **Tyre levers**
- **Puncture repair kit**
- **WD-40**

- Lubricant
- Solvent
- Grease
- Barrier cream
- Hand cleaner
- Third hand tool
- Shimano Pro-set tools
- Hammer
- Hairspray
- Tyre lever(s)
- Toothbrush
- Rock Shox pump
- Workstand

Almost all of these can be obtained from a good tool shop, the rest can be had from bike shops. (Except for the hairspray and toothbrush, more of these later.) Combination spanners have a ring spanner on one end and an open spanner on the other, and are the most versatile general purpose spanner. Socket spanners with extension bars and maybe even a universal joint are useful for getting into awkward places, and come in handy when you need to get two spanners the same size onto a cable clamp.

Alternatively, many bike shops

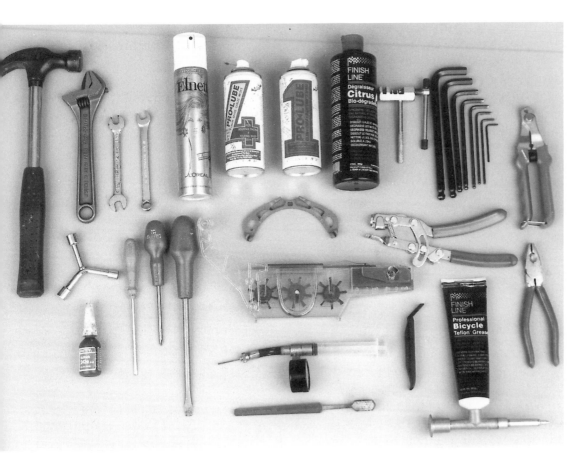

The basic, essential tool kit will allow you to replace, adjust and lubricate all the parts of your bike except the bearings. If all you ever want to do is keep your gears, brakes and transmission working smoothly, this is what you need stock a Y-spanner which has 8mm, 9mm and 10mm sockets in one easily handled unit. Other sizes of Allen keys than those listed here are sometimes encountered, though more often on accessories and ancillary components than on bikes themselves. These eight will do for almost all jobs on the bike itself, especially if you're only dealing with a standard SunTour or Shimano equipped bike; if you come across a component that needs an Allen key you don't have, take it down to your friendly local tool shop and make sure you get the right size. Unusual sizes of Allen keys are sometimes encountered on oddball American custom components, many of which require imperial size Allen keys.

If you add any super-light whizz-bang hyper-expensive parts to your bike (or, over-priced American rubbish as Brant would have it) make sure you get the right tools. By the way, the 8mm and 10mm keys don't properly belong here as they are needed to remove 1993 Shimano crank bolts and Shimano freehub bodies. However, you might as well get them while you are buying a set of Allen keys; it'll be cheaper than buying them singly later. We much prefer ball-end Allen keys, since these allow you to get at awkwardly placed bolts and are generally much easier to use. The small extra expense is worth it.

Combination pliers have a cutting edge and square jaws, with a rounded grip section in the jaws. Good cable cutters are a must. The cutting edge on pliers is not usually good enough

for brake cable, and tends to crush it. A bike shop will be able to get you a set of SunTour's excellent cable cutters, which are reasonably priced and will stand up to years of use.

A six or eight inch adjustable spanner is always useful to have in case you encounter an unusual nut or bolt size. Don't skimp on this tool good ones are a joy to use, cheap ones are nasty. Bahco make the best.

A cable puller, sometimes called a fourth-hand tool, is not essential (you can use pliers) but it does make the job of adjusting the tension in brake and gear cables much easier

A chain cleaner like those from Vetta and Park is the lazy mechanic's way of getting the dirt out of a chain; they're incredibly useful if you ride off-road a lot.

Tyre levers and a puncture repair kit can be obtained from bike shops, as can good quality water-resistant bicycle grease, like that made by Nimrod, Cyclon or Park, and a medium grade spray lubricant like Cyclon MTB, Superspray Lube MTB or LPS3. WD-40 is very useful for driving out water from splashed parts and releasing seized threads, but should not be used on its own as a lubricant; it's too light.

Solvents are a thorny issue. They are used to remove dirt which is too ingrained to wash off easily, but most solvents are toxic, both to people and the environment, and eventually they get washed down the drain. For this reason we try to use biodegradable chain cleaners like Finish Line, Pedros or Cyclon. Cyclon is claimed to be so non-toxic that you can drink it. We haven't tried it, but don't imagine that it tastes very good.

Barrier cream is available from auto supply shops and good tool shops. It forms a protective layer which prevents oil from soaking into your skin and clogging up your pores, and makes it easier to wash off afterwards. Good hand cleaner is essential; who wants to go around with dirt ingrained in their hands after a maintenance session? Swarfega is the most famous mechanic's hand cleaner, though Tufanega (from the same company) is very effective and less harsh on the skin. We used it in the bike shop where we learned bike repair because the head mechanic was allergic to Swarfega.

The correct Shimano Pro-set tool makes setting up any current Shimano brake much easier. A complete set is not expensive. We've moved the hammer to the intermediate tool kit because we've come across a really neat technique for fitting grips and bar ends that needs a hammer. It's a jolly useful thing to own anyway, and most households have one.

Hairspray is still one of the best things around for attaching grips.

Get plastic tyre levers; steel ones can easily wreck fragile alloy rims.

An old toothbrush is extremely handy when you need to get ingrained crud out of a part.

The only way to get air into a Rock Shox suspension fork is with the correct pump. If you don't have suspension forks you obviously don't need it.

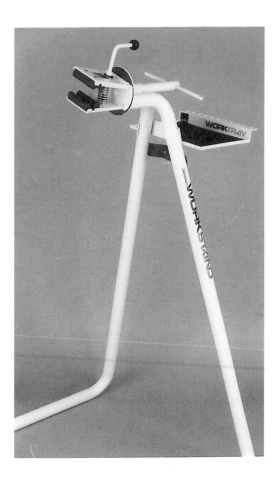

A good workstand is a very handy thing to have, but not utterly essential. Sooner or later, though, everyone who does a lot of their own maintenance goes out and buys one

We've left the workstand until last because it is not essential — you can lean your bike against the wall or turn it upside-down — but it does allow you easy access to all parts of the bike, making basic jobs like replacing gear cables much easier.

Having the bike held firmly is a real help when you get to the bearing adjusting jobs which the inter-mediate tool kit allows you to tackle. A couple of hooks on chains from the garage roof is a reasonable second best if you can't afford a workstand; it holds the bike up at a sensible level so you can work on it.

The intermediate tool kit

The next level of tool kit allows you to get at the bearings in the headset, hubs and bottom bracket to grease, service, and replace them. It also includes a tube cutter which is handy for trimming handlebars, and the necessary tools to get into a set of elastomer suspension forks to change the elastomer springs (often this is just a special Allen key).

These tools are relatively expensive and are not needed very often, unless you ride a lot, in which case they are an investment that will quickly pay for itself. Raleigh team pro Paul Hinton reckons that he completely rebuilds the bearings on his bike every month when the weather is bad. During one very wet summer, Paul was stripping and rebuilding bearings on a weekly basis, because every race happened under very wet conditions.

Being able to service the bearings will allow you to keep your bike in the best possible working order, and you will learn quickly when a component needs attention. Regular replacement of the grease in bearings will prolong their life, and save you money in the long run. These tools are:

- **Headset spanners (two)**
- **Fixed cup spanner**
- **Lockring spanner**
- **Adjustable cup (peg) spanner**
- **15mm pedal spanner**

- **Cone spanners**
- **Crank extractor**
- **Freewheel remover or Hyperglide lockring remover**
- **Chain whips**
- **Tube cutter**
- **Needle-nosed pliers**
- **Extra-long 5mm Allen key**

Usually, the first five of these consist of three double-ended spanners, which reduces the bulk of the kit a bit. The best and most expensive of these tools are those made by Campagnolo, Var, Park and Shimano. These are pro quality tools, and are probably overkill for a one-person home workshop, but if you're setting up a club tool kit which will be used by lots of people, then they are a worthwhile investment.

For a home workshop, look for the cheaper, but still reasonable quality, tools from Tacx and Madison, who also do peg and lockring spanners which are adjustable for a wide range of bikes. Although the Campagnolo patterns are standard on the more expensive mountain bikes, odd lockring and adjustable cup spanner sizes are sometimes found on cheaper and older bikes. In a club workshop, therefore, adjustable tools for these parts are useful.

Make sure that you get the right headset spanners for your bike. Road-size headsets, usually referred to as one-inch headsets because of the steering column size on the forks, need 32mm spanners, and are still

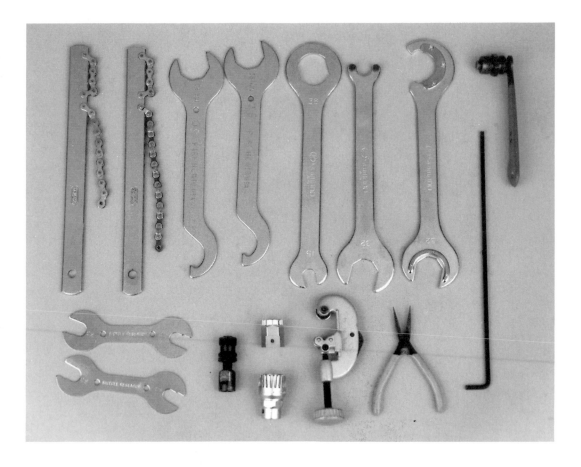

found on some manufacturers' mountain bikes. Tioga size headsets (1⅛ inch) need 36mm spanners and Fisher Evolution (1¼ inch) need 40mm spanners. The latter two sizes are referred to as oversize since they are larger than the standard one-inch road bike size which was universally used on mountain bikes before 1989.

The two oversize types have the advantages of longer life and greater strength, and the disadvantage of adding four more spanners to an already crowded tool kit.

Good, thin cone spanners are essential, and are not prohibitively expensive. You need a minimum of two 13/14mm spanners and two 15/16mm ones, or a pair of good multi-spanners like those made by Bicycle Research which incorporate all four sizes in one spanner. In addition a 17mm spanner for Shimano lock-nuts is useful, but it does not need to be a dedicated cone spanner.

Your crank extractor should be the same brand as your cranks, to ensure that it fits properly. Alternatively, a double-ended extractor such as Park's works on almost all Japanese and Italian cranks and will fit TA cranks should you ever run across them.

There are two systems of attaching

freewheels currently in common use, and they require different tools. Almost all Shimano-equipped bikes use their freehub system, where the freewheel body slots on to the hub, is held in place with an internal 10mm Allen key bolt and so needs a 10mm Allen key to remove it. A Hyperglide lockring remover tool is necessary to get the sprockets off first. Other freewheels screw on to the hub, and a special tool which fits into the notches or splines in the centre of the free- wheel body is needed to remove them.

Every other freewheel manufacturer makes its own remover; most of them are different and a complete set of freewheel removers runs to about a dozen tools. Fortunately, most bikes which have a separate freewheel have a SunTour or Shimano one, or clone thereof, and it is unlikely you will ever need any remover but these two. If you do, take your wheel down the bike shop and get the staff to order the right remover for you.

Chain whips are not part of some bizarre sadomasochistic bike mechanics flagellation equipment, but are used to remove sprockets from freewheel bodies, since they usually wear out first. Cyclo make basic ones that are OK for dismantling new blocks, and for holding Shimano Hyperglide blocks while you undo the lockring which holds them onto the freehub body, but for dismantling stubborn blocks better quality units like Tacx and SunTour are more reliable.

Eventually most pro mechanics end up making their own chain whips after they've broken a couple of sets on an extremely tight block. One of our mechanics got so fed up with breaking good chain whips that he ran up a set with two-feet long handles made from stainless angle iron and industrial strength rivets holding the chain. They worked.

A tube cutter does the tidiest possible job of trimming handlebars. It's not something you're likely to need often, but is a handy part of a club or team tool kit.

It's amazing how often you need to grip something small or get into an awkward place when dealing with bearings, which is why a set of needle-nosed pliers is included here. They are also the most useful thing for removing the Shimano crank dustcaps which have two little holes in them.

If you have suspension forks which use elastomer stacks as the spring- damping medium, then you are going to need to service them sooner or later, if only to switch the elastomers for harder or softer ones to fine-tune the ride. Pace, Manitou and Shocktech forks all need some sort of extra-long 5mm Allen key to achieve this.

Advanced tools

This is a small set and contains what *Bicycling* magazine once called 'the most dangerous tool known to man.' We're talking about a spoke key, which in inexpert hands can do more costly damage in less time than anything else in the tool kit.

The advanced tool kit contains the tools you need to true, repair and build wheels. This is a set of jobs which many riders prefer to leave to the wheel wizard at the local bike shop, but if you can true your own wheels they'll last longer. Some people find that they just don't have the patience, and that's a point of view that we can sympathise with; we true our own wheels when we have to, not out of choice. We'd rather be out riding than sitting at a wheel jig, but when there's no option but to true our own wheels we're glad that we can. The tools you need are:

- **Wheel truing stand**
- **Spoke key**
- **Wheel dishing tool**

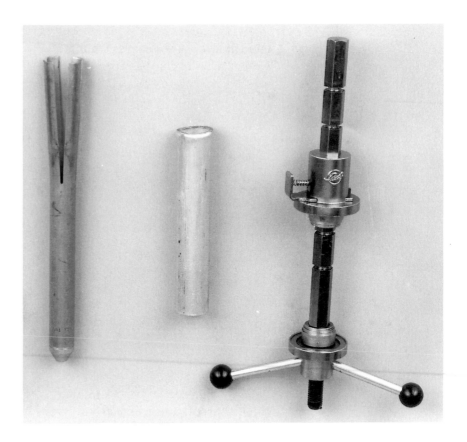

A good wheel truing stand makes the job so much easier that it must be considered essential if you've no experience with wheels. This is a bit of a paradox, because it is not a cheap tool. Before taking the plunge, see if you can borrow one; if you find you can't stand truing wheels, you haven't wasted any money. It is possible to use a bike frame as a rudimentary wheel stand, but it's less than ideal. A real wheel jig holds the thing securely and at the right height.

Get the best spoke key you can lay your hands on, like a Park, Var or Spokey unit. There are two common sizes of spoke nipple on mountain bikes, British and Japanese; make

sure you buy the right key for your bike. A spoke key should fit the nipple tightly.

A wheel dishing tool is necessary with most wheel jigs to correctly centre the rim on a rear hub, though the Park jig I use has a centring function designed in and therefore removes the need for a separate dishing tool.

Professional tools

The only pro level tools used in this book are a headset press, headset crown race hammer and headset cup remover (or rocket tool, so called

A headset press, rocket tool and, in the middle, an old bit of high-strength aluminium tube for use as a crown race hammer. These are professional tools that are virtually essential for replacing a headset, but few people could justify the cost

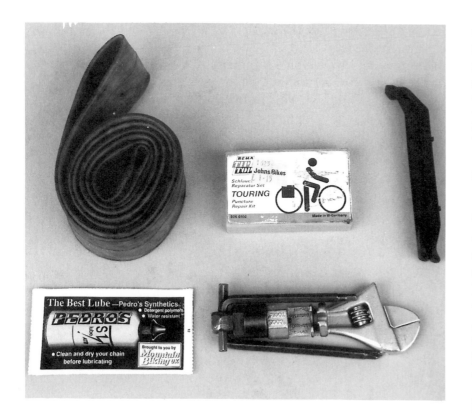

cutters (taps and dies), reamers, files and so on. If you are already a skilled metalworker, then you may find occasional use for these tools while working on your bike, but in the hands of a rookie mechanic they are likely to do more harm than good.

Trail tools

There are riders whose trail tool kit consists of nothing but a large dose of optimism. Faced with a wobbly component, miles from help, not having a tool kit will mean a long walk home. Whilst you could carry all the tools in your kit everywhere, there are a few that can safely be left behind. Here's what we carry when we go off road:

- **Cool Tool**
- **Spare tube**
- **Tyre levers**
- **sachet of lube**
- **Puncture repair kit**
- **Zip ties**
- **Spare 5mm, 6mm Allen bolts and nuts**
- **Pump (on the bike!)**

A Cool Tool is an amazingly handy device that includes 4mm, 5mm, and 6mm Allen keys, cross-head screwdriver, crank bolt socket, spoke key, chain tool, and small adjustable spanner. It replaces so many heavy tools that its asking price of about £20 makes it an absolute bargain.

because it looks a bit like a rocket if you squint at it from the north-west while the sun is low in the east, or something). These tools are included because they are an example of a job which is virtually impossible to do right without the correct tools. In this case the correct tools cost more than several new headsets, and no one in their right mind would buy one for home use; headsets just don't need replacing often enough to justify the initial cost, unless you are certain that your children and grandchildren are going to be keen mountain bikers in which case you can always leave it to them in your will.

Other pro-level tools are generally metal-working tools such as thread

The workshop

All you really need is enough space to work in, a table to clamp a wheel stand to and a tool-box to keep everything in. At home I take over the entrance hall, and pack my tools out of the way when I've finished, but at the *MBUK* office I have the luxury of a permanent workshop. This is really the ideal solution, and I tend to do most of my maintenance work at the office as a result. If you can afford to give over an entire room or garage to be a bike workshop, then you end up with a place where you always know where everything is, and you don't have to rummage through the entire tool-box looking for that 2mm Allen key because it's on its hook on the tool board.

Of course as soon as your friends get wind of this, they'll be round all the time to fix their bikes. The last time I lived in a house with a dedicated bike workshop it contained six people and 20 bikes. We were running two clubs and a racing team between us, and there was a fairly constant throughput of club members fixing their bikes. We had to keep a close eye on the tools; it's not that people will deliberately walk off with them, just that it's easy to absent-mindedly put an Allen key in your pocket when you've finished with it. If you find yourself with this problem paint all your tools an easily recognisable colour, or get them stamped with your initials.

The tool board

Having a dedicated workshop means that you can add a further tool to your kit, a tool board. This is simply a slab of chipboard, say about one by two metres, screwed to the wall, with enough hooks, nails and blocks of wood with holes drilled in them to hold all your tools. When you've found a place for everything, drawing round each item in indelible marker will make them easier to replace. The importance of having the right tools cannot be over-emphasised. Making do with a pair of pliers and a cheap adjustable spanner is a sure way to strip threads, round nuts and generally do expensive damage. The right tools make the job so much easier that they are a good investment just in terms of reducing hassle and frustration.

General hints and tips

There are a few general things about the engineering of bikes you should know before you start, and a few basic procedural rules you should follow to make life easy for yourself.

1 Grease all mating surfaces. These include threads, the handlebar stem where it fits into the frame and the seatpost where it goes into the seat tube. Grease stops corrosion and makes things easier to move. The only exception to this is on the

surfaces where the cranks fit on the axle; these should never be greased.

2 Threads are right-handed. With the exception of the fixed cup, left hand pedal and some internal threads in some Shimano pedals, all bike threads screw in clockwise and unscrew anticlockwise. Practise screwing and unscrewing a simple part like a bottle boss bolt until your fingers know this without you having to think about it.

3 Keep things clean and tidy. Clean tools, clean bike parts and, especially, clean lubricants all make for longer-lasting, more successful repairs. Don't let your tool-box get full of crud, and if your tools get greasy in use wipe them off with degreaser at the end of a session. If your grease gets contaminated, chuck it away and buy a new tub (better still, use a grease gun or tube of grease). Get into the habit of always putting tools back in their place as you use them, and divide your tool-box up according to which tools go where. Anyone who has seen either of us work will find this amusing, since we're not terribly organised mechanics, but a bit of order and tidiness does make any job lots easier, just because you don't waste time trying to find the 2.5mm Allen key you need for that American hub.

4 More confident mechanics might like to investigate the use of Loctite thread-locking compounds instead of grease in placements like cantilever brake anchor bolts. These anaerobic glues hold threads well enough so that they cannot shake loose, but will still come undone when you need them to. Use light grades like 222 and 242 as some of the higher grades are practically permanent. A good tool shop will be able to advise.

3: CLEANING

Everyone remembers their first mountain bike. After every ride you clean and polish it until it looks like new, recoiling in horror from a small scratch in the top tube. The fact is that you don't have to keep your frame tubes bright and sparkly to make your bike ride better, but it is essential to ensure that the moving parts — brakes, chainset, wheels, and so on — are clean. Apart from anything else, it's impossible to perform any maintenance on your bike if it's inches deep in soil samples.

It makes sense to keep your bike clean. Proper cleaning will help prolong the life of your bike, but done wrongly it can cause more damage than leaving it dirty. Other chapters in the book deal with cleaning specific components; what we deal with here is the routine cleaning you should do after every grubby off-road ride.

How much do I have to do?

How much time you spend on your bike's personal hygiene is up to you, but we regard time spent polishing the paintwork as time wasted. We could be out on the trail for longer! If you're not happy unless your bike has a deep down showroom shine, then fine, but you don't have to do it.

The minimum that you should do after a ride is important. If you've just hosed off the dirt, relubricate the chain and look at the cables occasionally. Dirty chains wear sprockets and chainrings very quickly. A little attention can save a lot of money.

Hosing

With the increasing popularity of jetwashes found on petrol station forecourts, and even available now as a do-it-yourself accessory, it may seem tempting to blast the dirt off your bike, rather than spend time scrubbing it. Jet washes certainly are effective in removing farmyard debris and grimy muck from your frame tubes, but their high pressure spray is far more than the seals on your bearings can stand. As a first step, the jetwash is a great way to clean a lot of the heavy muck from your bike, but there are cheaper and more efficient ways of cleaning the cack from your frame.

If you are going to use a jetwash, don't spray directly into any bearings. The lip seals stand up OK to water trickling off them, but the considerable pressure from the hose will soon work its way into the bearings.

An excellent story appeared in a US mag a couple of years ago when a rider, visiting Durango, Colorado, came upon another mountain biker casually jet washing his bike at a garage. When it was pointed out to him that maybe he should be a bit more careful, since the pressure could easily damage bits of his bike, the happy jetwasher just said, 'Yeah, but I guess I get a new one pretty often.' The visitor then realised he'd been giving a lesson in bike washing to world champion Ned Overend. Unfortunately not all of us have an unending supply of free bits, so we need to take more care.

The pressure supplied by a normal garden hose isn't as bad for the bearings, but it is still worth taking care, and not flooding the key bearing areas with water. Hubs, bottom brackets, headsets and suspension forks can be cleaned with a hose, but point the spray away from directly contaminating the bearings.

Bucket and brush

A far safer and cheaper method of cleaning your bike is to use lots of warm soapy water and a stiff bristled brush. To do this properly, you can remove the wheels from the bike, which gives you access to the tricky bits and allows you to clean corners around the rear mech and bottom bracket and under the fork crown.

Start by giving the whole bike a good scrubbing from the top down, cleaning any debris from the tyres and brakes, before working down to the drivetrain. It's OK to use a garden hose for this, but keep the spray away from the bearings. Once large amounts of superficial dirt have been removed, you can concentrate on cleaning individual parts properly.

Before you do this, use a fine mist spray from the hose to clear all the cack from the bike, which will loosen up the dirt further and make cleaning of the rest easier.

Using a stiff bristled hand brush, dipped in biodegradable solvent or really soapy water, you can clean the heavily gunked up parts of the bike without transferring too much of the dirt to yourself. Give the chain a quick clean and then spend a little

Don't spray water directly into the bearings, or else the grease could be forced out, and the bearings will rust. This isn't a problem of course, if you're going to repack everything, but if you're not, don't do it!

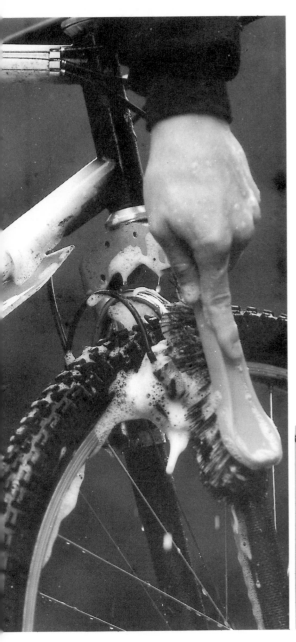

more time getting the dirt off the front and rear mechs and sprockets. Get the muck out from between the sprockets, and you'll be amazed at how much better your gears shift. The less greasy grime you have here, the less dirt your bike will pick up.

Pay particular attention to the parallelograms that operate the gear mechanisms. Once the pivots of these get dirtied up, they require much more thumb pressure to actuate a change.

Chain cleaning is far more easily and effectively completed with a special chain cleaner available in several different varieties. Just add the degreaser, spin the pedals round, and the chain is clean for relubing.

Relubricate the cables by removing them from their slotted stops, and running thin oil into the housing. GT85, Pedro's or Finish Line lube

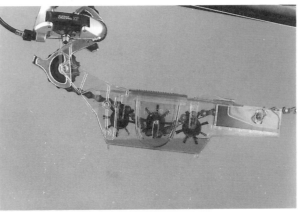

A stiff bristled brush is my favourite way of getting everything clean, along with lots of soapy water. Any soap will do, car stuff, pots and pans stuff, not oven cleaner

A chain cleaner gets your chain looking good again easily. Just put in the cleaner, stick your chain through the myriad of rollers, and spin the cranks. Hey presto, a clean chain

It's that stiff brush again, doing its business getting the freewheel clean. Removing the cack from between the sprockets improves shifting and drivetrain life no end

Don't go spraying gallons of lube all over your bike. You'll waste a fortune, and everything will be sticky. It's far better to just lubricate the bits that need it

is most suitable. Never use grease on gear cables as it blocks up the housing. Also lubricate the pivots on the front and rear mechs. Spray specific areas, rather than covering the whole mech with oil. It attracts less dirt and costs you less too!

Brakes

Brakes don't require such a thorough cleaning as the drivetrain, as they don't get as dirty. Open the quick release, give the pads a scrub with the bristly brush, checking that there are no spiky objects in the grooves of the block trying to score concentric circles in your rims.

Just as you relube gear cables, the brake cables do require some attention as water ingress causes rust, and this will mean the cables don't run smoothly from lever to pad.

Grease is used for brake cables because of the higher loads involved. Put a pinch of grease between your thumb and first finger, and slide it

into the cable, where the housing goes.

Suspension Forks

It's advisable, as with any type of sealed component, not to squirt high pressure water onto the seals of suspension forks. This could drive water inside, and stop them working well. Clean suspension forks with a sponge, removing the muck from the top seal. For a detailed description see Chapter 11 on Suspension.

Need to do more?

This is all you'll have to do after the most muddy of rides, but if you've really not cared for your bike, then you may need to service a part more thoroughly.

Cleaning the bike lets you get the muck off the surface and actually see the components. Now you're in a far better position to check the integrity and wear of the parts.

4: TYRES, TUBES AND PUNCTURES

The variety of tyres available for mountain bikes now is vast and bewildering, but the one thing that all of them have in common is that sooner or later they will puncture. Even the best puncture resistant tyres, which have Kevlar belts under the tread to stop thorns or other debris from penetrating through to the tube, are susceptible to impact punctures, so fixing a puncture is probably the most basic skill a cyclist needs.

That said, there are mountain bikers who lead an utterly charmed life and just don't get punctures. Australian mountain bike champion Tony Smith turned up in Britain a few years ago, on his way to the World Championships in Switzerland, and took in a round of the Shimano Series – the first British Championship series. He rode the two hundred miles from Heathrow to the race venue in County Durham, raced, then spent the next few weeks riding round Britain, then on to Switzerland, all without a single puncture. Good job too, since we later found out that he didn't know how to fix one!

Unfortunately, come the Worlds, Tony got fairly badly knocked about when he crashed after puncturing and had a long walk back down the mountain to the finish line.

Ask most bike shop mechanics to repair a punctured inner tube for you and you'll get a funny look, with usually a straight refusal. Patching a tube just isn't worth the effort; at their hourly rates it's cheaper to fit a new tube than to try repairing the old one. The same is true of fixing a flat on the trail. There's absolutely no point trying to repair a tube if it's wet and cold, and even if it's fine, you don't want to hold everyone up while you wait for the glue to set. No, the thing to do is to carry a spare tube, and replace the punctured tube with a fresh one. Fix the punctured tube when you get home.

This sounds pretty obvious, but there are some techniques that will speed up the process. These are especially useful to racers, but recreational riders can also benefit from fast tube replacement; who wants to spend time fixing a tyre when they could be riding?

Component selection

The secret of fast tube changes is to carefully match tyres and rims. We used to run Mavic M6CD rims for fun and recreational riding. At 490g each, they were by no means the lightest rims around, but they had two big advantages: they were tough, and their deep shape meant that tyres came off them really easily. Racing on M6CDs, 89 National Champion Deb Murrell astonished spectators by pulling her punctured back wheel out of her bike and ripping the tyre off with her bare hands.

Easy, if you know how, and the way how is to use M6CDs or another rim that allows quick tyre removal. Our current favourite rim choices include Campag's oddly named but excellent Atek and Stheno, Ritchey's Vantage, Bontrager BCX-1s and -2s and other rims that have a deep well which allows the tyre bead to move into the well and get out of the way.

Choice of tyre is important too, some will come off easily, some need tools. If your choice of tyres is down to a few, then take a wheel into the shop and select the tyre that most easily comes off your rims.

We also use slightly undersized inner tubes, so that the tube doesn't impede tyre fitting or removal. 1.5inch butyl or latex tubes stretch quite happily to fit two-inch tyres. Polyurethane tubes however, don't stretch and must be sized accurately. We mention them only for completeness, however; they seem to have all but disappeared from the shelves. For reasons that we'll get to later, they were never a great idea anyway.

The worst rims we ever came across for getting tyres off were the old Mavic Rando M4s. You needed steel tyre levers or an unending supply of plastic ones, since they usually snapped, thumbs as strong as Arnold Schwarzenegger's arms, and friends with very broad minds about swearing! We have seen Taiwanese tyres that are almost as bad on shallower modern rims.

To fix a flat fast all you need, if you've chosen tyres and rims carefully, is a pump or gas canisters and a spare tube. I carry 1.5inch Presta tubes as spares, so that I can lend a spare to anyone else who punctures. Presta valves will fit through a rim thats drilled for Schrader, but a fat Schrader valve won't go through a Prestá-sized hole. Some tyre/rim combinations allow you to literally just pull the tyre off the side of the rim. If your tyres are a tighter fit, you'll need tyre levers. Use plastic ones, not steel, and especially not your mum's spoons. Plastic levers are less likely to damage the rim and tube as you remove it.

We've broken the apparently simple process of changing a tube down into a large number of steps because there are a handful of tricks that we've learned over the years that make the job a lot simpler and quicker if you use them. British resident, New Zealander, and pro racer, Paul, 'I ride for Raleigh,' Hinton is famous for the speed of the tube changes he manages in races using these techniques.

Changing a tube

Open the wheel quick release and drop the wheel out of the frame (for notes on using quick releases see Chapter 8). It can still be awkward to get a fully inflated tyre through a brake, but since we're talking about a flat tyre here, it's not a problem. If it is, open the brake quick release by squeezing the blocks together and pulling the straddle or link wire out of the brake arm it hooks into. If it's a rear wheel, put the gear on to the smallest sprocket, open the quick release, pull the mechanism back out of the way and drop the wheel out.

Front wheels just drop out of the fork, unless you've got safety dropouts in which case you'll have to unscrew the quick release lever a few turns to get the wheel to drop out, making it into a slow release. Racers tend to choose forks without safety dropouts or grind them off; when you're in a hurry, they're a pain.

If there's any air left in the tyre, let it out. To do this, remove the dustcap and depress the centre of a Schrader (car-type) valve. For skinny Presta valves unscrew the top bit (it's a locking collar) and push it down to release the air. Then push the valve into the tyre to allow the bead to move on the rim without the valve holding it in place.

To get a slack tyre off the rim, push the bead away from the edge of the rim, into the well, right round the circumference of the rim. This liberates all the slack that's available. Grab the sidewall with both sets of fingers and thumbs, with your hands about three inches apart. Pull the bead up out of the well and pop it out over the edge of the rim. Gradually work your hands apart, pulling out more and more of the bead until you can just slip your finger under and pull it off the rim.

Most tyres are a slightly tighter fit than this, and need one tyre lever to get them off. Very tight tyre/rim combinations need two tyre levers. Lets deal with the single lever technique first:

One lever tyre removal

With practice you will be able to perform this process in one fluid motion; insert the lever, pull up the bead, push the lever round the rim, pull off the tyre. In races this is a critical technique.

Pumps and canisters

Some puncture kits come with rather small gas canisters, but there are now huge 25g Air Zefal cartridges available. These will get a two-inch tyre up to full pressure in seconds, but they're a fairly expensive way of fixing a flat — worth it for racers, but probably a bit over the top for casual riding. Our favourite pump is still the Mt Zefal Plus. We've lost them, but we don't know anyone who's managed to break one or wear one out yet.

Put the punctured tube in your tool bag and take it home for later repair. To get it down to the smallest package possible, roll it up while holding the valve open.

Push as much of the tyre bead as possible down into the rim well, and lift the bead away from the rim at one point

The lever goes in with the curve uppermost as shown. This may seem painfully obvious to experienced riders, but we've seen rookies try to use levers the other way up simply because no one had ever shown them the right way to do it

Ease the lever under the bead to lift it. Take care not to catch the tube as you slip the lever under the bead — you don't want to add another hole to the one you're already going to have to fix

Push the lever as far as possible round the inside of the rim to lift as much bead as possible over it. This step is impossible with tight tyre/rim combinations, at which point you know you're going to need two levers. Now push the lever along the rim, levering it up and down as you go

Two lever tyre removal

Very tight rim/tyre combos will require two tyre levers to get them off. The right way to use a pair of tyre levers is to first slip them both under the bead, four to eight inches apart, next to the spokes. If you put one lever in and hook it to the spoke it will pull the bead so tight that it'll be very difficult to get the next lever in

Then, flip one lever at a time to lift the bead over the rim, and hook one lever on to a spoke

Push the loose lever (the one that's not hooked on to a spoke) away from the hooked lever to lift the tyre of the rim. This should be easy, and if it's not, it's time to switch to a looser tyre and rim set

Pull the inner tube out and run your hands around the inside of the tyre until you find the cause of the puncture. This may be a bit of glass, so don't feel for it too vigorously or you'll cut your fingers. If you can't find the cause, don't worry. If the puncture was very rapid it was almost certainly a snakebite impact puncture

Partially inflate the new tube, just enough so that it holds its shape. Experienced riders, and those in a mega-race-type hurry, can omit this step, but it does help prevent the tube from getting pinched by the tyre

Put the valve through the valve hole and put the tube into the tyre. Push the tube over the rim so that it sits in the rim well and the loose tyre bead sits next to the sidewall of the rim

Starting from the valve, lift the bead over the sidewall and push it down into the well, pulling the slack round the rim as you go. Make sure the valve is pushed well into the tyre so that the area by the valve doesn't get pinched by the bead and puncture

The last few inches are the hardest. Work them on gradually by gripping the body of the tyre and pulling the beads on with your thumbs. This takes practice, but you should be able to fit even the tightest tyres without recourse to tyre levers. Put the wheel back in the frame before inflating the tyre. This saves you the hassle of opening the brake

Pump up the tyre (we've left it off the bike for clarity). Racers use gas canisters, the rest of us carry pumps

This is a good way to store any tube; the less space your tube takes up the more room you have in your bum bag for tools, Mars bars, satellite navigation systems. If you carry two tubes, wrap a re-usable zip tie round the punctured one so you know which it is.

Impact Punctures

Impact or 'snakebite' punctures can be dangerous. A sudden front tyre puncture at high speed usually causes a disastrous loss of control which is a good reason for keeping your speed sensible on steep downhills.

Snakebite punctures are caused by the inner tube being pinched between the tyre and rim when the tyre bottoms out against the rim as it hits a rock or other obstacle. They leave a characteristic double hole in the tube, hence the name, and can be prevented by keeping tyre pressures fairly high, or using the fattest tyres you can fit into your frame.

If the flat was very slow the cause may be a very fine piece of wire or thorn. I once spent two months replacing tubes every other ride until I finally found the thin wire strand that was causing all the flats.

If you're having this kind of problem, there are only two ways to cure it: either replace the tyre, or spend as long as it takes going over the tyre with a fine tooth comb until you find the offending object. A bright light helps, as does locating the hole in the inner tube, and thus narrowing down the area of the tyre you need to investigate.

Repairing the puncture

Puncture repair kits have improved to the point where a good puncture repair can be regarded as permanent, so it's worth fixing the tube. You need a puncture repair kit like the Tip Top, Specialized or Nutrak ones. Here's how:

Pump up the tube so that it is about two inches across, if you're using a track pump, go carefully; it's quite easy to completely destroy a tube by over-inflating it until it explodes, and I know people who've done this while chatting away as they inflated a tube. Saves fixing it, I suppose.

To find the hole, pass the inflated tube near to your face and listen for the hiss of escaping air. If this doesn't work, the hole is very small and the way to find it is to minutely inspect the tyre by eye.

Eventually you'll find the hole by getting a thin jet of air in your eye, though this can take some time. The foolproof way of hunting for a hole in a tube is by passing it through water, but this has the disadvantage that it leaves the tube wet, and you've then got to dry it before you can fix it. However, it is a useful last resort when searching for the tiny pinholes that cause maddeningly slow punctures.

Inflate the tube gently to test the seal and leave it for an hour or so, so you can tell whether it's going down. Don't inflate it humungously hard; if you pump it up to above its normal inflated size, you can blow off even the best patch.

Choosing tubes and tyres

There is a huge range of tyres on the market, and several different types of inner tubes to go inside them. It's not possible to give details of them all here, not least because by the time this book appears there will probably be a dozen new ones on the market which we don't know about yet!

The simplest choice is of inner tube. Broadly there are three types, standard butyl rubber, which is black and is the most common by far, natural latex rubber, usually coloured blue or pink, and polyurethane, which is nearly clear in colour and much stiffer than the other two.

Butyl tubes have the advantage of being cheap, very widely available and fairly easily reparable. We like Michelin's 1.5inch butyl tubes, which are of consistently good quality and fairly light, and Specialized's. Check the length of the valve if you are using narrow, deep rims; some valves do not leave enough shaft protruding from the rim, making them impossible to pump up.

Latex tubes are a relatively recent innovation in mountain bikes, though roadies have been using them for years.

Latex is much more flexible than butyl rubber so it tends to give rather than tear when confronted with a sharp object and this makes latex tubes more puncture-resistant than butyl ones. Because most puncture repair kits contain glue that is intended to work on natural rubber rather than butyl, latex tubes are somewhat easier to repair than other types. Latex tubes tend to be a bit oversized, so it is sensible to use the smallest ones you can find. However, latex tubes do seem to have a problem: as they stretch to fill a tyre, some of the tube can stick to the inside of the casing, while part of it expands more to fill the well of the rim. This section can then stretch permanently, become weakened and subsequently tear. To prevent this, use lots and lots of talc to lubricate the tube inside the tyre.

Fixing a patch

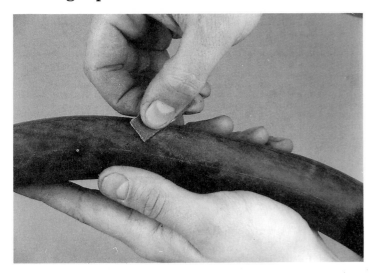

Mark the hole by roughening the area around it with the emery cloth or sandpaper from the puncture repair kit. As soon as you deflate the tube, the hole will vanish. Even snakebites can become hard to find and pin pricks are all but impossible unless you know exactly where to look — so keep an eye on the location

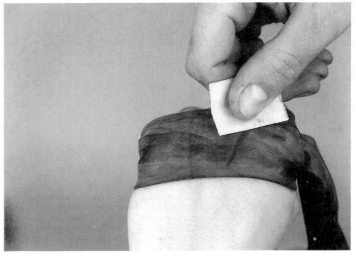

Deflate the tube and wrap it round the back of your hand to give you a firm surface to work against. Roughen an area of the tube about twice as big as the patch — this is an essential step because it vastly increases the ease with which the patch will stick to the tube

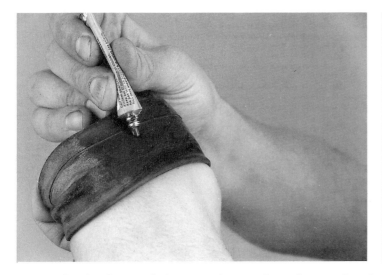

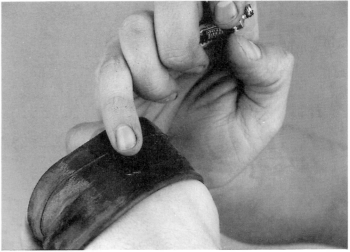

Spread a thin layer of glue over the roughened area: the glue needs to be practically dry before you apply the patch, so give it a few minutes to get tacky. Go and make a cup of tea or something; the glue won't go completely dry unless you leave it for hours, but it does need to be tacky, not wet

Peel the backing off the patch (the silver foil not the clear plastic). Keep this patch surface clean; it won't stick if you get grease or dirt on it, so hold the patch by the plastic backing rather than the middle

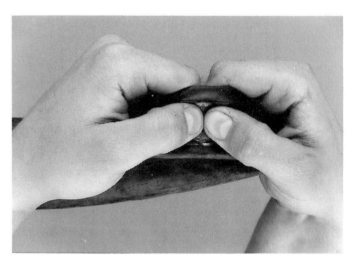

Position the patch over the hole and press it firmly on to the tube. Putting the tube under a pile of books to hold the patch on firmly will allow you to do something more exciting while it sets. Give it at least several minutes to set

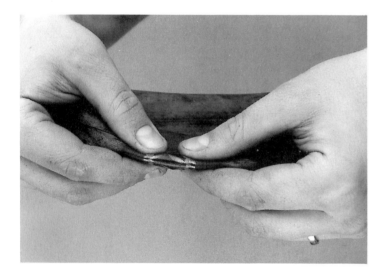

Fold the patch over in the middle to crack the plastic, peeling the plastic off from the centre outwards. If you peel from the edge, you will probably lift off the edge of the patch as well, so don't!

Polyurethane tubes came and went around 1989-91. The toughness of the material helps reduce punctures, but they are hard to fix when they do puncture and a special repair kit is needed. They are usually lighter than butyl tubes, but must be an exact fit in the tyre, because they don't stretch much when inflated. This can make them awkward to fit, to say the least. John once spent half an hour trying to wrestle a polyurethane tube into a tyre that it was supposed to fit, before giving up in disgust and using a butyl tube! Frankly, polyurethane tubes aren't worth the hassle.

Tyres

Your choice of tyre depends on a number of factors including the type of surface you usually ride on, your weight, your riding style and how much you are prepared to risk reliability for speed if you're racing. One complication of choosing tyres is that the markings on tyre sidewalls do not accurately reflect the size of the tyre. A batch of tyres from different manufacturers, all marked 26 x 2.0, will differ by as much as 6mm in the actual width and depth of the tyre. Since it is the width and therefore the air volume of the tyre that determines how well it will cushion the rim and rider, it would be useful for this information to be accurate.

There are moves afoot among tyre manufacturers to introduce a standard system of markings which will give the tyres actual width in millimetres. For the moment, however, you may as well disregard the sidewall measurements and go on how fat the tyre looks — it's about as accurate.

The thinnest off road tyre currently available is Specialized's 1.5inch Hardpack. This is useful for very light, smooth racers on relatively smooth courses with no significant high-speed descents, but does not really provide enough protection from impact punctures at sensible pressures for it to have many other applications. The fattest rubber is the 2.5inch Ground Control Extreme, also from Specialized which provides outstanding traction and cushioning, but is a little heavy for many riders tastes. In between is a huge range.

It goes without saying that the thinner tyres, usually nominally 1.9inch wide, will be lighter and therefore accelerate and climb better. However the problem with such tyres is that they are prone to bottoming out and developing impact punctures, unless you keep them pumped up fairly hard. This in turn reduces traction and comfort, and is really only a practical compromise if you're racing, and you're fairly light.

Most riders use slightly larger tyres, nominally 1.95, 2.0 or 2.1 inches, and good brands to look out for include Specialized, Onza, Ritchey, Tioga, Kona, Marin, Panaracer and Michelin. All these manufacturers have their own ideas about tread patterns, but there are some general principles that apply to all tyres.

The tread of a tyre basically consists of two areas: the centre, which is in contact with the ground when the bike is going in a straight line; and the edges, which come into play in cornering. Widely-spaced treads work well in mud, while tighter treads are better in sandy soils and on dry, hard-packed dirt.

Tall, well-supported side lugs give good cornering, though if they are too tall they will fold and the tyre will slide. Tread compound makes a difference to tyre performance, especially in the wet, as well as to durability, and manufacturers are always trying to balance grip and longevity. The ultimate high-traction tyres were the limited run of white rubber Onza Porcupines which were used in downhill racing, but the tread compound was so soft that they had to be replaced after a few races. This sort of design is clearly not practical for most riders, whose wallets will not run to frequent tyre replacement, so most manufacturers use tread compounds that afford less traction but better durability.

Soft treaded tyres like standard Onza Porcupines and Panaracer Smokes are superb off road, but tend to wear quickly if used on tarmac. More durable tread compounds are used by Specialized and Ritchey, whose tyres are more suitable for multi-purpose use.

Hard-core riders and racers may have several different types of tyres for different terrain, but equally many riders use the same tyres no matter what. One thing is for certain; you don't have to stick with the same kind of rubber that your bike came fitted with. The best source of information as to which tyres work well in your area is your local mountain bike shop; a bike shop staffed by mountain bikers is an invaluable resource.

5: TRANSMISSION

The transmission, which consists of the chainrings, gears and chain of your mountain bike, is the most complicated single system on the machine and also accounts for the largest number of moving parts on any bike. Transmission parts are relatively expensive and tend to wear out much more quickly if not kept clean and well-lubricated. The most important component of the transmission is the chain.

The chain

Mountain bike chains have a ridiculously hard life. We expect them to transmit pedalling effort, shift easily from sprocket to sprocket when we want them to, but stay put when we don't, last forever, and do it all covered in highly abrasive dirt.

Well, the good news is that, by and large, chains work incredibly well, especially if they get the right sort of tender loving care and you're careful about little things like splitting and joining them.

Because the chain is far and away the most exposed of the bike's moving parts, it picks up more grime than any other. This grime contains silica, the basic mineral from which rock and soil are formed. Silica particles are considerably harder than steel bike chains so tiny particles of it in the links of the chain act as grinding paste, wearing away the bearing surfaces. After a period of time this wear, accumulated over the chain causes it to become longer.

Sprockets and chainrings are designed to be used with chains that have their rollers exactly half an inch apart, and such chains are referred to as half-inch pitch for this reason. There are advantages to smaller pitch chains, such as the 10mm system Shimano attempted to introduce for track and road bikes a few years ago, but the half-inch pitch is now so entrenched that it will remain long after everything else in bicycles has gone metric. No one will ever talk about 12.7mm chains!

Anyway, the point we're getting to here is that a worn chain has rollers spaced fractionally more than a half-inch apart. This means that all the load on the chain goes through one roller, one sprocket and chainring tooth at a time, rather than being spread over several of each. This accelerates wear on the sprocket and chainring teeth causing them to become hooked and eventually so worn that a new chain slips over them and the whole bang-shoot, sprockets, chain and rings, need replacing at once. This is an expensive business and can be delayed by diligent chain maintenance. If you don't clean anything else on your mountain bike, you should at least clean the chain.

Cleaning and lubrication

Most riders hose their bikes down after a ride; keep the water away from the hub, bottom bracket and headset bearings and this works fine. Hosing is probably the best way of shifting superficial mud from the chain and getting it clean enough so you can clean it properly, or in other words, removing enough of the coarse mud off the top to get at the fine stuff underneath.

The fiddly way to clean a chain is to split it, take it off the bike and soak it in solvent. This is possible for most chains but the narrow chains on all Shimano Hyperglide-equipped bikes are not amenable to this kind of treatment, for reasons that will become apparent later.

A Hyperglide chain needs to be cleaned in situ and this can be done by scrubbing it with a stiff paintbrush, then an old toothbrush, and solvent such as Cyclon or Pedro's degreaser (both biodegradable, a major plus). You can run it through a Park or Vetta chain cleaner: these are plastic solvent baths which clamp round the chain as it runs through solvent between brushes, which scrub out the grime. A really grubby chain will take a few goes through one of these devices to get it properly clean, needing fresh solvent each time. This is the easiest way to clean any chain. Be careful if using diesel as a solvent; it's harsh on sensitive skin, so use

barrier cream. **Do not** be tempted to use petrol; you could blow yourself up.

Since whatever you use is going to go down the drain eventually, you should use a biodegradable solvent anyway.

After you've got it clean, lubricate it with a thick spray oil such as Super Spray Lube MTB, Rockoil or Pedro's Synlube. The easiest way to lubricate a chain is to hold the spray can still and turn the pedals quickly backwards to pass it by the lubricant spray. Sounds obvious, we know, but we have seen people use a whole can of lube in one go, trying to pass the can along the chain and get into the fiddly bits around the rear mech and chainset.

Removing the chain

A chain needs replacing when 12 full links measure 12⅛ inches long. Any longer and there will be wear on the sprockets and chainrings as well, necessitating their replacement.

There are now several nifty tools on the market that indicate when a chain is worn. Get one, they can save you money in the long run.

If the chain is slipping on the sprockets or chainrings, then it is way past time it was replaced and you'll need new chainring sprockets as well. I once acquired a Trek bike that had done a 5,000 mile expedition and the transmission was completely shot because the rider, reasoning that chains are heavy things to carry as spares, had simply not bothered to replace it when it got worn. The middle ring was completely shot, and the cassette and chain also needed replacing. The total bill was nearly three times the price of a replacement chain.

To replace the chain you first have to get it off, and of course you might want to remove it to clean it. To do this, you need a chain splitting tool, as sold in bike shops everywhere. Most chain splitters have two sets of locating plates for the chain. The one furthest away from the punch is for splitting and rejoining it, and the other nearest the punch is for adjusting a stiff link.

We still hear of people asking for split links for derailleur geared bikes, but unfortunately, although they do exist, they don't work. The kind of split link which old three-speeds used to have, which you prise open with a screwdriver, will spontaneously prise itself open as it passes through the jockey wheel of a derailleur, and so can't be used. To break a derailleur chain, you need a chain splitter.

Pull the chain through the front and rear mechs to take it off the bike. To clean it, dump it in a tin of solvent and leave it to soak for half an hour, then, if youre using Cyclon or Pedro's chain cleaner, rinse out the solvent under the tap and hang it up to dry. Lube it and hang it up so that the excess lube can drip off.

To re-fit the old chain, thread it through the gears and position it on the splitting and joining plates. Push the pin back into the chain until it just protrudes from the opposite side. To cut a new chain to the right

Place the splitter on the chain with the chain on the splitting plates and turn the handle to push the pin partially out

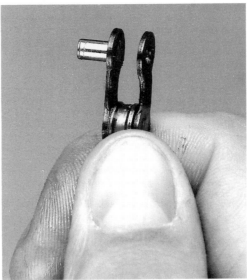

Don't push the pin all the way through; push it out so that it is retained in the outside plate. Trying to replace a fully pushed-out pin is possible but difficult. If necessary, back the punch off and try to part the chain after every turn

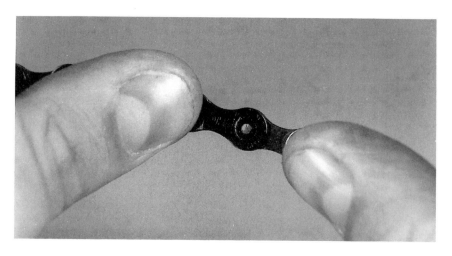

If the rejoined chain clicks as it goes through the gears, the joined link is stiff. To cure it, either push the pin through or back a fraction on the stiff link removal plates of the chain splitter, or use simple brute force; grab the chain with your fingers and thumbs and flex it from side to side

length, simply lay the new and old chains out next to each other, so that they start at the same place, measure the length of the new chain off against the old and cut the new to length with the chain splitter. Hyperglide chains should only be trimmed at the end which does not have a pin sticking out of it.

Hyperglide chains

These chains are found on almost all Shimano-equipped bikes since 1989. They are joined by a special black link which has oversized ends. This link should not be used to split the chain. The HG chain can be split anywhere except at the joining pin, which, having oversized ends, will damage the chain as it comes out.

A new HG chain must be joined with a pin which comes fitted to its open end, so don't take this off when trimming it. Shimano make special pins for rejoining chains, which are available from Shimano Service Dealers. The old pin should be

pushed right out and the new pin, which has an extended pointed end to locate it in the chain, used in its place. The extended end should then be broken off with pliers.

All of this is necessary because HG chains have the links peened over to prevent them coming apart under the strain of normal use, but paradoxically this creates a problem when you actually want to take them apart. As you push out the pin it leaves a large hole in the plate which does not properly hold the pin when its refitted. Consequently, the chain spontaneously parts when you're riding. I had a Hyperglide chain which not been joined properly (I installed it before Shimano realised they had a problem with this design) and it came apart with monotonous regularity. I reached the point where I didn't go anywhere without a splitter, and got very good at recognising the noise the chain made just before it came apart.

The joining pin which the chain comes with and the special pins which must be used to rejoin the chain, have oversized ends to prevent this problem. Although this seems on the surface to be a lot of hassle, it is very rare for a properly joined HG chain to come apart in use, and if they are cleaned and maintained well, they are fairly durable.

Joining a Hyperglide chain

If all this does seem like a lot of unnecessary hassle, Sedis' excellent SL chain works perfectly with Hyperglide (and all other) gear systems, needs no special pin and can be easily removed for cleaning.

The rear derailleur

Most engineers find the humble rear derailleur a pretty offensive device. You see, chains just aren't meant to derail; in virtually every other application of a chain as a drive mechanism it sits permanently on two sprockets. If gears are needed they are achieved by systems of gear wheels that are independent of the chain, like those in a motorbike gear box. These systems aren't practical on bicycles because they're heavy, or at least the standard system of derailleurs and multiple sprockets is lighter. In many engineers' eyes, though, the amazing thing about modern derailleurs is not how well they work, but that they work at all!

If it's a genuine source of amazement that derailleurs continue to work when covered in a mixture of heather, leaf-mould, mud and sheep debris, then it's no real surprise when things go wrong, but a little simple cleaning and preventive maintenance will stop most problems before they start.

Cleaning

There are riders who like to go around with a layer of crud on their bikes to prove it gets off-road but they still need an efficient gear-shifting system, and that means a clean one.

Hose the mud off as usual. Clean

Put the joining pin into place in the chain, thin end first. Push the pin through in the normal way, until the end you're pushing on is just proud of the link plate

Break the thin end of the pin off with pliers. Adjust stiff links as above if necessary

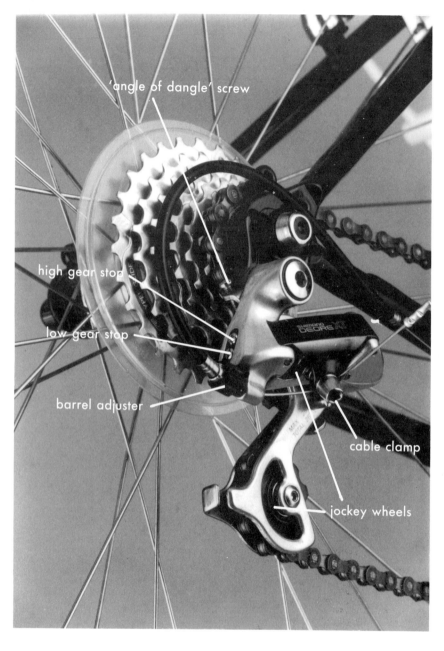

'angle of dangle' screw

high gear stop

low gear stop

barrel adjuster

cable clamp

jockey wheels

Rear mech

and lubricate the chain, then scrub off any remaining mud with an old toothbrush and solvent. Lubricate all the mech's moving parts: jockey wheels, springs, pivots and cables. Sticky and kinked control cables are a major cause of hassle with indexed gear systems; if in doubt, replace them. Get the original manufacturer's cables if you can, but if not, Clark's make excellent replacement gear cables.

Adjusting the rear mech

There are three adjusting screws on a rear mech: the bottom two limit the in and out movement of the mech; the top one adjusts the tension of the top spring, which in turn affects the angle at which the rear mech hangs (Shimano call this the b-tension adjustment screw, but we call it the angle of dangle screw) and the barrel adjuster on the cable outer trims the indexing by changing the tension in the shift cable.

To adjust the rear mech if it goes out of sync, first get the top and bottom gear stops properly aligned:

The angle of dangle screw is used to adjust the trim of the mech so that the top jockey wheel moves as close as possible to the sprockets for efficient shifting, without rubbing on them. If the top jockey rubs on a sprocket, turn the angle of dangle screw until it doesn't.

Once the stops are adjusted, use the barrel adjuster to trim the indexing. If you're not sure just what the barrel adjuster does, try rotating it a turn in each direction and note the effect on the indexing.

Adjust the top stop screw so that the chain runs smoothly on the smallest sprocket; the top jockey wheel will be directly below the sprocket when this happens. If the mech won't go all the way out to the sprocket, it's possible that the cable is too tight, in which case screw in the barrel adjuster to slacken it

Shift into the biggest sprocket and adjust the screw so that the chain remains on the sprocket and cannot fall off into the spokes. Some manufacturers use a spoke guard to prevent this happening, but if your gears are properly adjusted it's not necessary. It's possible for a chain to rip through the spokes and demolish the wheel if it comes off the sprocket, so take extra care with this step

Indexing adjustment varies between SunTour and Shimano mechs. A SunTour mech needs to be adjusted so that it shifts smoothly between the first and second sprockets, a Shimano one so that it just fails to over-shift from second to third. For SunTour tweak the barrel adjuster a half-turn at a time, then try the shift until it makes the shift from first to second cleanly

For a Shimano mech, put the chain on the second sprocket and screw the barrel out until it begins to get noisy when turned, then screw it back in until the noise stops. It should now index properly

Replacing a rear mech cable

The cable is attached to the rear mech by an Allen bolt or a nut, depending on the make and model of derailleur. Virtually all current SunTour or Shimano rear mechs use a 5mm Allen bolt to fix the cable, though some cheaper models use a nut. A cable needs to be replaced if there is any sign of fraying or kinking damage. Similar damage to the outers means they need replacing.

Undo the bolt and if there is a cable end cap, pull it off with pliers. Pull the cable out of the cable outers at the rear mech, shifter and seat cluster (if the cable is top routed). Depending on the type of gear system you've got, here's how to get the cable out of it.

Original Shimano Deore XT and Deore DX STI Rapidfire gear shifters had a small cover plate which needed to be taken off before the cable could be removed. If you have these shifters, unscrew the cover plate. Put it somewhere safe; it's dead easy to lose. Then, as for all Shimano shifters that aren't top-mount thumbshifters, push the upshift button six or more times, until the head of the cable is visible in the window, and push it out of the shifter. If you can't see the nipple after pushing the top upshift button several times, put the cover plate back on and take the bike to a dealer. All Rapidfire shifters are sufficiently complicated that further disassembly is unwise, to say the least, and best left to expert mechanics.

Pre-1993 Rapidfire shifters below DX in the Shimano range have a large hole in the body which the cable can be pushed through when the shifter is in its highest gear position.

SunTour's ill-fated X-Press shifters are now rare. If you have them you need to undo the central screw on the underside of the shifter and take off the cover plate. This is made from fairly soft plastic and can therefore be flexed to get it off the shift levers; it's not unbreakable, though, so be gentle with it. The cable end will now be visible in the metal section, which the levers are attached to, and can be pulled out. For some reason SunTour chose to use a different shape of cable end from everyone else. Rather than have the cable attach to the end of a cylindrical nipple, SunTour attach it to the side, so you do need a specific SunTour replacement cable.

Getting a cable out of a thumbshifter is easy; just pull it out. The various double-button shifters Shimano and SunTour have perpetrated in the last few years are more complicated

If you need to replace the cable outers, now's the time to do it. No index system will work properly without the right outer cable, properly prepared. Get Shimano SIS (or SunTour, or whatever) outer cable, cut it to length with Shimano's cable cutters, so that it travels in smooth, short curves to the stops. Re-shape the ends with the handles and fit Shimano's own end caps. Don't try to use brake outer, or anything else that looks like it will do. It won't.

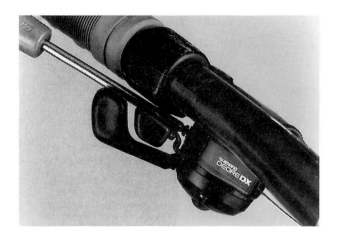

Jockey Wheels

Take a look at the condition of the top jockey wheel. Shimano top jockeys are supposed to have a small amount of side to side movement, but they should move sideways

Top: original Shimano Deore Dx and XT Rapidfire shifters have a cover plate which needs to be removed to get at the gear wire. Don't lose the little screw

Middle: current (1992 XTR and XT, and all after 1993) Rapidfire Plus shifters have rubber plugs to do this job. You probably won't be able to find them on your shifter, because they fall out extremely easily. Again, pull the upshift trigger until the head of the cable becomes visible, and push it out

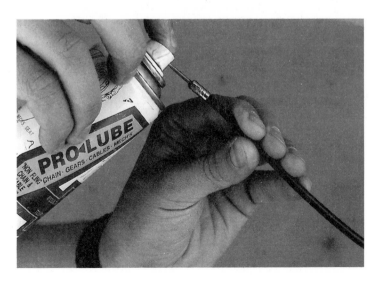

Right: fill the outers with a thin, slippery lubricant, such as Superspray MTB Lube or LPS. The little tube that comes with some brands of lube is very useful for this

Pull the cable taut with pliers or a fourth-hand cable puller and tighten the cable anchor bolt. Pull the bare cable at the down tube, or top tube, sideways by hand to pre-stretch it, and take up any slack that is generated by loosening off the anchor bolt and repeating the last step

Far right: the finishing touch is to crimp a cable end cap around the end of the cable with pliers. As well as looking neat and tidy, end caps make it possible to reuse a cable should you have to dismantle the transmission for some reason

smoothly and not rock around the clamp bolt. SunTour top jockeys are not supposed to move sideways, but experience has shown that SunTour's gear systems often work best when the top jockey has developed a small amount of sloppiness.

If the top jockey seems to be excessively worn, replace it. Bear in mind that you should get the manufacturers own replacement top jockey; SunTour and Shimano jockeys are not interchangeable.

Routine maintenance

After initial setting up, the only adjustment aside from lubrication that a rear gear needs is to take up the slack in the cable. Unscrew the barrel adjuster a little after the cable has had a week or so to bed in.

Replacing a rear mech

A rear mech needs replacing if it gets thoroughly mangled in an accident; the most common mech killer is a large twig caught in the transmission or rear wheel, which yanks the mech out of line and bends it as it goes. American mountain biking writer John Olsen, who rides in the forests of the US Pacific North West, reckons to get through two or three rear mechs a year — British trails tend to be a bit less hazardous!

When a rear mech gets written off it tends to damage something else in the process, usually the chain, which gets twisted, or the gear hanger. A twisted chain is incurable and must be replaced, but a bent hanger on a steel frame can be bent back into place. If the gear hanger is bent the new mech will not hang straight, but will lean towards or away from the spokes. Special tools are available to align the rear mech, but with practice it can be done with a couple of 12inch adjustable spanners.

Aluminium hangers cannot be realigned because aluminium work-hardens when it is bent. This means that it becomes brittle very easily, so is much more fragile after it has been realigned. Most manufacturers of aluminium frames now get around this by using a bolt-on gear hanger which can be replaced if it gets damaged. Here's how to replace a rear mech:

Undo the cable from the rear mech, remove the cable end cap if there is one and pull the cable out of the mech.

Undo the bottom jockey wheel to allow the chain to be removed without splitting it

Undo the rear mech from the frame (usually requires a 5mm Allen key). Strip the old rear mech for spares like cable adjusters, screws, bolt and jockey wheels

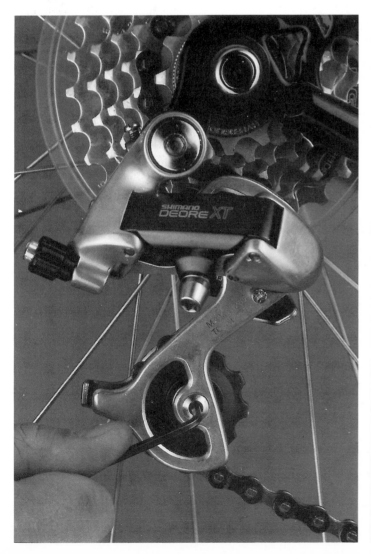

The front derailleur

If engineers find rear gear mechanisms offensive, then front derailleurs can only be described as crude. A front mech simply shoves the chain across from one chainring to another by the unsubtle method of hitting it with a steel plate. Sophisticated it ain't.

Nevertheless, front mechs have come a long way from the first designs which appeared in the thirties. The earliest front mechs consisted of two parallel plates that simply pushed the chain sideways from ring to ring. As a result they had a very narrow range, as little as eight or ten teeth, and didn't work spectacularly well. The best modern mountain bike front derailleurs can cope with a total difference between chainrings of 26 teeth, and will shift in pretty appalling conditions. All you really need to do is keep them clean, well lubricated and well adjusted.

Lubricate the mech and cable frequently. If your bike has slotted cable stops you can get at the inner to lubricate it really easily; put the bike in lowest gear, then move the shifter to its high-gear position to generate slack in the cable. You will now be able to pull the cable out of the stops and wipe lube on to it with a clean, lubricated cloth

It has to be said that the technique of straightening the gear hanger requires more than a little skill and sensitivity, and is best left to a pro mechanic unless you are confident of your abilities when it comes to the controlled bending of bits of metal.

Grease the thread and screw the new rear mech into the gear hanger. Hold the rear mech up so that the plate next to the attachment screw fits behind the stop on the hanger. Reconnect the cable and fit a fresh end cap, as explained above.

If you have managed to twist the gear hanger out of alignment, this is how to straighten it. Clamp two large adjustable spanners at 90° to each other — one on the dropout, the other on the hanger — and use them to bend the hanger back into line

Cleaning

After you've hosed off the inevitable mud (taking care to keep the water away from the nearby bottom bracket bearings) any well-attached dirt can be scrubbed off with solvent and an old toothbrush. Front mechs rarely malfunction because they are dirty, but cleaning them allows you to check the condition of their various parts, especially the two plates that form the cage. Eventually most front mechs break, because one of the plates wears out from the continual abrasion of the chain during shifting. It's worth keeping an eye on the condition of the plates; if they look excessively worn, replace the mech.

Front cable replacement

Most of the problems that arise with front mechs are the result of the cable getting sticky, and the simplest way to cure the problem is to replace it. It is possible for a badly neglected front mech to seize up (see below), but its rare. Removing the old cable from a front shifter is much the same as from a rear shifter. Pull off the cable end cap, undo the clamp bolt and remove the cable from the shifter. See Rear mech cable replacement above for how to get the cable out of your particular shifter. The left-hand, front mech shifter has the same cable attachment system as the right-hand rear mech unit. If the cable won't come out, refer the problem to a

Cable end cap · Big ring adjusting screw · Cable clamp bolt · Little ring adjusting screw · Outer cage plate · Frame clamp bolt · Inner cage plate

dealer; dismantling STI units is a job for experienced mechanics only.

Fill the cable outers with thin lube, thread the cable through them and the frame stops and connect the cable to the mech. Pull the cable tight, do up the clamp bolt, and cut the cable to length with cable cutters. Put a cable end cap on the cable and crimp it on with pliers.

Front mech adjustment

Front mechs have four adjustments, angle, position (height), big ring limit and small ring limit. In addition, indexed front derailleurs need precise adjustment of the cable tension to

Some Shimano front mechs, particularly on oversize frames, use an endless band clamp. These are fitted by undoing the Allen bolt, taking off the clamp and reassembling it around the seat tube.

Check that the front mech shifts quickly to the big and small rings in all the gears, and especially that it drops to the small ring from the middle ring when the rear mech is on the largest sprocket. If it won't, you may need to adjust the small ring limit screw to allow the chain to fall a little further so it engages the small ring. You will also need to loosen the clamp bolt and release a small amount of slack cable so the mech can move down. Make this adjustment a small amount at a time, so that the chain does not end up falling off the inner ring.

Adjusting STI front indexing is basically a matter of setting the cable tension so that the chain falls from the big to the middle ring when the downshift button is pressed once. (This is the upper button on original Rapidfire and the finger trigger on Rapidfire Plus.) To do this, put the chain on the big ring, then press the downshift button. The chain should drop smoothly to the middle ring.

If it overshoots, unscrew the barrel adjuster on the shifter to tighten the cable. If the chain doesn't drop to the middle ring, screw the barrel adjuster in until it does. If there is insufficient adjustment possible, loosen the clamp bolt, screw, the adjuster out to create some slack, then retighten the cable and adjust accordingly.

The front mech should be positioned so that the outer cage plate clears the big ring by about 2mm, when you move the mech up to the big ring position. If you have elliptical rings, the mech should clear the highest point of them by about 2mm

align them on the middle ring. I've always felt that front indexing was a solution in search of a problem, but most manufacturers seem convinced that we need it, so we need to know how to tweak it.

If you're fitting a new front mech, there is no need to split the chain. Instead, undo the screw that joins the two halves of the cage and slip the mech over the chain. Replace the cage screw and tighten it. Clamp the mech loosely to the seat tube.

Let the mech spring back to the little ring and put the rear mech in the largest sprocket. The chain should just clear the inner plate on the front mech.

Use the small ring limit screw, the innermost of the two adjuster screws, to adjust it. If you're fitting a new mech, attach and tighten the cable at this point

The outer plate should be parallel to the big ring when viewed from above. With the mech correctly positioned, tighten the clamp bolt. Sometimes a mech will shift position slightly as the clamp bolt is tightened. If this happens, note how much it has moved, loosen it off, move it the same amount in the opposite direction to compensate, then tighten it up.

All that remains is to adjust the limit screws to stop the chain from falling off the big and small rings, and tweak the cable tension so the front indexing, if any, is accurate

Put the front mech on to the big ring and the rear mech into the smallest sprocket. The outer plate should just clear the chain. If it doesn't, use the big ring limit screw, the outer of the two screws on the top of the mech, to move it in or out as necessary

Seized mechanisms

Front mechs do malfunction if they have not been kept lubricated, and the simple symptoms of this are that the mech seizes up or becomes very stiff. A very stiff front mech action may also be the result of cable or shifter problems, so to check the cause, disconnect the cable at the mech by undoing the cable clamp bolt, and try to move it by hand. This will require quite a lot of force, since front mechs have strong springs, but it should be possible. If it is not, the mech is seized.

To free up a front mech, you need to take it off the frame. Undo the frame clamp bolt and the cable clamp bolt, if you haven't already, then take out the little screw which holds the cage plates together. This will allow you to flex the plates far enough apart for the chain to slip between them, and it is less hassle than splitting the chain. Put the cage screw back in, so you can't lose it.

Soak the mech in the thinnest penetrating lubricant you can find, like WD-40, Duck Oil or Super Spray Lube and leave it to creep into the pivots for a few hours. Then attempt to move the cage again. It should now be possible to get the mech to move a little, and repeated applications of penetrating oil and brute force should eventually restore it to full, free mobility. If it won't free up there's no option but to throw it away and get a new one.

Routine maintenance

All a front derailleur really needs is to feel loved; keep it clean and lube the pivot points and cables regularly and it'll last ages. To lube the cables, put the mech on the big ring, then set the shifter to the small-ring position. This creates enough slack to allow you to pull the cables out of the slots in the stops. Wipe them with a clean rag soaked in lubricant.

6: BRAKES

Far and away the most common type of brake found on mountain bikes is the cantilever. These brakes are actuated by a cable which runs from a lever on the bars to a brake caliper, which consists of two pivoting arms bolted on to bosses on the frame, located on either side of the wheel. The brake cable splits just above the tyre and pulls each arm up and inwards equally to pull the blocks into the rim. This type of brake has the advantages of excellent mud clearance, simplicity, light weight, ease of maintenance, and when designed and set up properly, great braking power.

About five years ago, Shimano introduced a different design, the U-brake, which was basically a very beefy version of the old centrepull brake, long popular with cycle tourists. Unfortunately its mounting position, under the chainstay, gave rise to a heap of problems with clearance and mud-clogging and it was soon abandoned. At the time of writing it is not possible, as far as we know, to buy a U-brake equipped production bike. The section of U-brakes in this chapter has therefore been shortened, and anyone who still has one is best advised to seek the advice of a good dealer about spares availability and repair.

In the meantime, various means have been introduced to improve the efficiency of cantilever brakes, and Magura's Hydrostop hydraulic brakes have acquired a small but loyal following, not least for their virtually maintenance free operation. The maintenance changes that this has brought about are covered here, from Shimano's M-System brakes to additional rocker systems as used by Cannondale and Pace Research.

Cantilever brakes

The switch from heavy, indifferently functioning hub brakes to light, efficient cantilevers was one of the things which transformed the original California clunkers into proper mountain bikes. Since then, cantilevers have evolved from the Mafacs that were all there was in the early 80s to the sophisticated stoppers of today like Shimano's Deore XT M-System units.

Cleaning and general care

Spray water at 'em! Happily, cantilever brakes have no inconvenient, fragile bearings that will get destroyed by the slightest ingress of moisture. Actually that's not quite true, since they do have steel springs and bronze bushes which could conceivably get seized up. When you've washed off the mud, spray the pivots with a thin penetrating lube (LPS1, Superspray Lube, Cyclon) to drive out any water that's crept in.

While you've got your can of lube in hand, spray a little on the pivot point in the lever to keep it moving freely, and lube the cables. This is easy if your bike has slotted cable stops as most now do. Unhook the straddle cable quick release (QR) to produce some slack, pull the outer away from the stop, move it along the cable and lube each bit as it is exposed until you've done the whole cable. The easiest way to lube the exposed cable is to spray some on a cloth and use that to wipe the cable. Put the outer back in the stops and reconnect the QRs. When you've got them clean, it's time to check the brake blocks for wear and tear.

Most blocks have little water-dispersing grooves cut into them, and the manufacturers say you should replace them when the block has worn to the bottom of the grooves. This usually means throwing away a brake block which has half its useful pad material left, but since most brake blocks consist of pad material moulded around a metal body, it is essential to replace them before they get down to the metal, since these metal cores can seriously damage rims. It is better to err on the side of caution and follow the advice given by the manufacturer.

Blocks can also damage rims if chips of rock or metal get embedded in them and score the sidewall of the rim. A chunk of rock can do irreparable damage fairly quickly, so it's worth checking the blocks for particles quite often. To do this, push them into the rim, pull out the straddle wire and allow the brake to spring open. You can now see the braking surfaces and should dig out any intruding objects with a sharp implement.

Servicing cantilevers

All of the routine jobs you might need to do on a cantilever brake — cable replacement; block replacement; lubing a sticky pivot; general adjustment — make up a complete service on the brake. We've therefore dealt with the complete job of servicing a standard brake system in the following section.

Removing the caliper

All cantilevers have a wire arrangement in which a bolt in one arm of the brake clamps a wire, while the other arm has a quick release which just pops in and out of a hook at the top. To get a complete brake caliper off the bike, unhook the quick release, pull the cable end cap off the clamp arm with pliers, undo the clamp and undo the bolts which attach the arms to the frame.

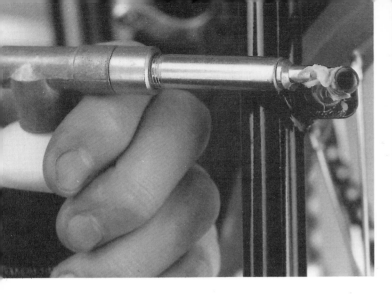

For most brakes it's important that the brake bosses are lubricated so that the brake arm moves smoothly on the boss. Recent Shimano brakes have a built-in bearing that removes the need for this boss to be in perfect condition, but a little grease on it will stop it rusting anyway. If the brake does not move easily on the boss, clean it gently with fine emery paper, checking the fit frequently until the arm turns easily. The problem here is usually a little leftover paint on the boss

Remove the cover on the back of the arm to expose the spring. Note the position of the spring in the cover so that you can put it back in the same place when you replace it. It's unusual for the coil springs in cantilevers to cause problems, but a dab of grease on them will stop them from corroding. If the springs are exposed to the elements, common on cheaper cantilevers, this is an essential precaution

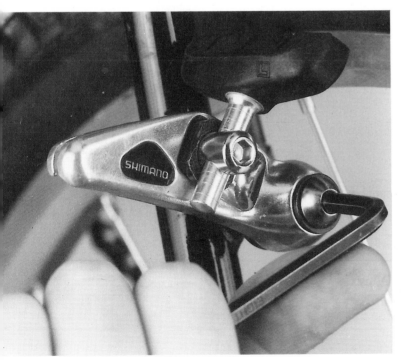

Put the brake back on the boss. Most bosses have three holes in the back plate. Put the spring in the middle hole unless you want to alter the spring return action. For a stronger spring return, which also means more force at the lever to pull on the brake, use the bottom holes and for a weaker action use the top holes.

Dia-Compe and SunTour brakes usually don't use the back plate holes. Instead they have an internal spring tension adjustment system, which requires a cone spanner to be used to turn a nut behind the brake arm. You might notice that the bolt has bits of blue stuff on it from the original assembly. This is thread-locking compound to stop the bolt working loose. It's not essential, but you might want to try replacing it with a light grade of Loctite.

More recent Shimano brakes (1993 and 1994 M-system models) use a piece of thin outer over the main wire to help adjust them. This piece of outer is exactly the same length as the link wire and so removes the need for all that faffing about with pro-set tools. All you do is adjust the position of the top of the link wire so that the lines on the link wire nipple and link wire top are lined up, tighten the cable, then adjust the brake blocks so that there is 1-2mm clearance between block and rim

Most recent Shimano levers use this arrangement to anchor the cable, a pivoting piece to take the nipple, rather than a slot and hole in the lever itself. Take care to put the nipple all the way into the anchor piece; if it's only in halfway it is possible for the nipple to bend the thin pressed steel sides of the piece

These brakes use a cross-head screw to adjust the spring tension, not an Allen key

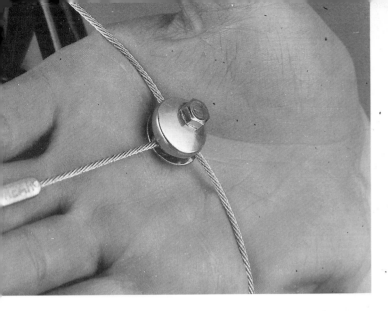

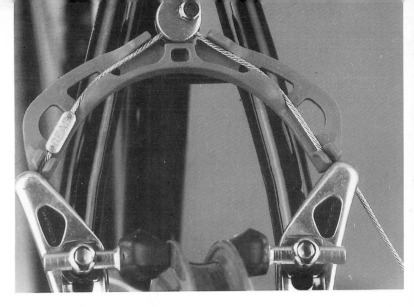

Shimano's direct wire cable linkage has become the most common configuration on recent bikes. There are several different version of it; this is the type seen before 1993, in which a clamp anchors a short link wire to the main cable, which in turn clamps into the clamp arm of the brake

To set up a Shimano link wire system quickly and easily to Shimano's specs, you need a Pro-set tool that is correct for the particular brake you are working on. There will be a number on the wire that corresponds to the number on the correct tool. Clip the tool to the cable between the cantilever arms, pull the cable tight through the clamp and tighten the bolt

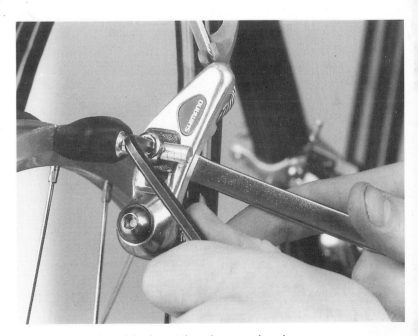

If there is one, tighten up the link wire clamp. On more recent brakes, all that will be necessary is to pop the main cable over into the little notch in the back of the link wire top piece

Position the brake blocks so that they are hard up against the rim, with the pro-set tool still in place. The clamp that holds the blocks takes a 5mm Allen key at the front and a 10mm spanner at the rear.

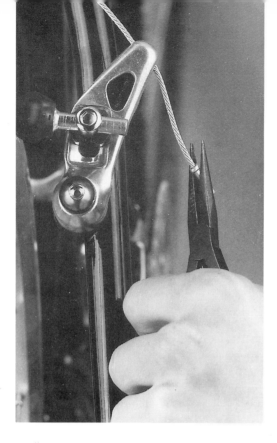

Trim the cable with cable cutters if necessary, fit an end cap and tuck the end of the cable behind the brake arm

Older cantilevers

Some older Shimano, SunTour and Dia-Compe brakes used blocks which are attached through a slotted plate with a nut, rather than having a stud that fitted into a clamp. These designs tended to work indifferently at best, and the correct replacement blocks are now hard to find. While it goes against the grain to recommend an upgrade just because spares for the old stuff are hard to find, the best thing you can do if you have such brakes is to up grade to a modern design, which you will find works much better.

Remove the pro set tool and use a 2mm Allen key to balance the spring tension of the two cantilever arms and therefore tweak the position of the blocks. Dia-Compe and SunTour brakes have a large nut behind the brake arm to adjust spring tension. To use it, slacken off the brake arm anchor bolt and turn the nut with a cone spanner, then retighten the bolt

Brake cables

Cables should be replaced if they are showing any significant signs of wear or fraying. If in doubt, replace them. There have been a few nasty accidents recently when front brake cables have broken, allowing the straddle wire to fall on to the front tyre and stop the bike abruptly, catapulting the rider over the bars. Leaving a fork-mounted front reflector in place will prevent this, as will regular cable maintenance.

Switching to beefy 2mm cables like Clark's, Shimano's or Odyssey's will improve braking power and feel, though they do need their own wide outers which may not fit the stops and levers on some bikes.

When replacing brake outer, cut it to length, aiming to run it in smooth curves with no sharp turns. Use proper cable cutters rather than pliers, (SunTour and Shimano both do good ones). File the ends of the outer smooth to remove any burrs the cable could snag on. Fill the outers with lube, using the little tube that comes with the can.

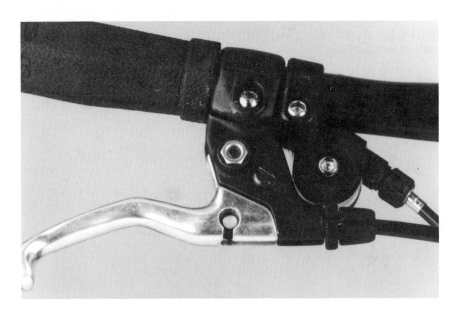

The underside of the Shimano Deore DX brake lever. Its reach can be adjusted by the slotted screw shown here

Brake levers

Most brake levers have an alloy body which clamps to the bar and is tightened with an Allen key. Pre-STI Shimano Exage levers have a cross-head screw inside the lever body. Brake levers need to be tight, but not so that they break rather than move in a crash.

Virtually all levers have some sort of adjustment for the distance from the lever to the bar. Pre-STI XT and DX levers have a four-position adjuster under the lever, all others have a screw on the inboard side of the body which needs either a screwdriver or the appropriate Allen key. The lever position affects the cable adjustment, so set it first, before changing the blocks or cables.

Dia-Compe brakes tend to use a

6mm Allen key. Each pad should have the same amount of stud protruding from the clamp. The pads should be angled so that the front edge of the pad hits the rim just before the rear edge. This is known as toe-in, and helps prevent the blocks from squealing. The pro-set tool curves the link wire and main cable just enough that the blocks will clear the rim when you remove it.

Magura Hydrostop brakes

Fitted to some 91 Saracen bikes, and available as an after-market upgrade, the Magura Hydrostop brake is one of the most powerful and

After filling the syringe with proper Magura fluid, the bleed screw at the brake pad should be loosened and removed with a 4mm Allen key

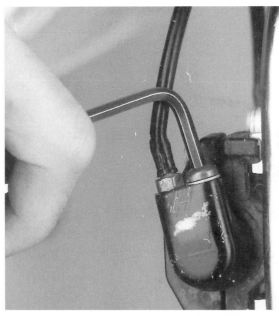

controllable brakes on the market. The huge benefit of this brake is its practically maintenance free operation. Changing the pads is simply a matter of pulling out the old pads, and pushing new ones in their place. Adjusting pad-to-rim spacing is a case of turning a small Allen screw in the brake lever to force the fluid through the lever, setting the pads closer to the rim.

Replacing a line is very simple, just a matter of having the right bits, as you need to form a compression joint to hold the line in place. After cutting the line to the right length, slide a compression olive in place. Use a new one every time, don't use the same one again.

Bleeding a hydraulic system is a matter of replacing the dirty fluid with clean, whilst ensuring that no air bubbles form. This is rarely necessary, only when the system has been contaminated with a broken

The syringe should then be placed in the hole, with the rubber seal firmly inserted. Pressure can then be gently applied to the syringe, whilst the bleed screw at the brake lever is loosened, and removed

Push the syringe, and keep pushing until clean, bubble free hydraulic fluid comes out of the brake lever hole. If this isn't possible with one pass of fluid, replace the lever bleed screw and refill the syringe then repeat the procedure. When clear fluid is finally passing through the system, the brake lever bleed screw can be replaced and tightened. Now the syringe can be removed without the worry of air bubbles forming. Refit the bleed screw at the caliper, and the brakes are ready to ride.

hose. Make sure that no brake fluid runs onto the rim, causing braking problems. It's not something that you need to do every weekend, I do it about once a year to check on the brake's condition.

U-brakes

Most of the maintenance requirements of U-brakes are the same as cantilevers. They can be safely hosed clean, with a little water-displacing lube sprayed round the pivots afterwards.

One occasional problem with U-brakes is that mud can accumulate between the arms of the brake, and the blocks. If mud in these areas has dried on to the point where it won't wash off, scrape it out with a screwdriver. Hard, dried mud on the blocks of U-brakes seems to be a cause of worn tyre sidewalls, so it is important to keep them clean.

All Shimano U-brakes use bolt-type blocks. Shimano's own blocks are practically essential as replacements for Exage brakes, which require very deep blocks, but good aftermarket units like Aztecs and Kool-stops will fit Deore brakes. Shimano U-brakes have no toe-in facility built into the brake, so it is necessary to get blocks which have curved washers to allow you to toe them in.

The old blocks will undo with a 10mm spanner; replace them when the water-dispersing grooves are worn out, or shortly thereafter. Undo the brake's quick release first, so that fitting the blocks will not be impeded by the cable, which will probably be shorter than necessary, and screw the barrel adjuster on the

brake lever all the way.

Slip the new blocks into the slots in the brake arms, position them approximately correctly, and gently tighten the nut to hold them loosely in place. Try to reconnect the straddle wire at this point, and if it won't reach, loosen the cable clamp bolt on the yoke and let enough cable through so that the straddle will reach.

Tighten the yoke cable clamp bolt very firmly. The easy way to adjust the toe-in on Shimano and Aztec blocks is to put a couple of pieces of thin card under the rear edge of the block and set the block up so the card is held in place when the lever is pulled and the front edge of the block touches the rim. With practice you can gauge this amount of toe-in by eye, though holding the brake in place can be awkward.

The block should be positioned as high as possible on the rim, because U-brake blocks tend to move up the rim as they wear and can end up filing the sidewalls of the tyre, resulting in an expensive and dangerous blow-out. Check the block position every time you take up the cable slack. All Shimano U-brakes use a 2mm Allen key in the left-hand side brake arm to adjust the spring tension and therefore the spacing of the blocks.

The straddle wire is exactly the same as a cantilever straddle wire, and is best run as short as possible to increase brake power. Bear in mind that GT bikes and clones thereof need the straddle wire to cross over around the plastic cable guide on the seat tube, otherwise the rear brake will not work properly.

7: CHAINSET AND BOTTOM BRACKET

Your feet rest on pedals, the pedals are attached to cranks and lurking between your feet is the bearing the cranks run on, the curiously named bottom bracket. The complete set of cranks, chainrings and bottom bracket is called a chainset and it all turns on the bottom bracket bearing.

The bottom bracket

All your pedalling effort goes through the bottom bracket and there is a school of thought that considers it to be the most important bearing on the bike. It's certainly one of the most annoying if anything goes wrong with it, since a loose bottom bracket is one of the main sources of mysterious clicking and creaking noises during pedalling.

There are now three types of bottom bracket. The most common on recent mountain bikes, in the mid to higher price bracket, is Shimano's cartridge type bottom bracket, which incorporates in one unit the axle bearings and threaded housings to fit into the frame. Not to be confused with cartridge bottom brackets which are a complete unit that screw in place to do the job of a bottom bracket. Cartridge bottom brackets look very like a normal (cup and cone) bottom bracket, but have cartridges holding the bearings, rather than loose balls. It is difficult or impossible to get at the internals of these bottom brackets to service them, and Shimano had considerable reliability problems with early versions. While the current ones seem reliable enough, we have to admit to a cordial dislike of any bike component that can't be serviced. Shimano introduced these bottom brackets for the convenience of bike manufacturers (they need no adjustment and are extremely quick to fit into a frame) not for the benefit of riders and mechanics who have to deal with the real world of mud and water which gets into any bearing and needs to be purged from time to time by dismantling and re-greasing. FAG and Tioga also make what are effectively cartridge bottom brackets as did SunTour.

The most common type of bottom bracket, simply because it pre-dates Shimano's switch to cartridge units and there are millions of them out there, is the cup and cone type. This has separate axle, bearing balls and bearing cups. The two bearing cups screw into the frame and an axle with curved bearing surfaces sits in between them, supported by the bearing balls. This system has the advantage that, with the right tools, it can be easily dismantled and serviced.

Less common, but gaining popularity with enthusiasts, is the cartridge bearing bottom bracket. This resembles a cup and cone unit, except that the bearings are contained in one-piece, ring-shaped cartridges which incorporate balls and bearing surfaces, and usually have steel or neoprene seals to keep out crud, which is why they are commonly referred to as sealed bearings. The cartridges are usually a tight press-fit on to the axle and into the cups; maintenance consists of carefully removing the seals to grease them once in a while, and replacing the cartridges when the bearings get worn.

Since the axle doesn't incorporate a bearing surface, it is possible to make such brackets with titanium rather than steel axles, which saves weight on your bike and your wallet. It's also possible to incorporate ultra-high quality long-life bearings, such as those used by Royce Racing in their superb £120 unit. As Royce once told freelance MTB journalist Mark Severs when he asked how to replace the bearings: 'You don't. When they wear out your grandchildren can send the unit back to us and we will replace them free of charge.' Confidence indeed!

Some cartridge bearing bottom brackets, like those used by Fisher and Klein, have the bearings directly fitted into the frame and held in place with circlips, which makes for very easy disassembly and servicing,

but many, like the Royce, are not suitable for home servicing. If you are thinking of going for one of these units, hang on to the service instructions that come with it; there just isn't room to go into all the possible variations here.

Axle types

The cranks are held on to the axle by either nuts or bolts, depending on whether the axle has an internal, threaded hole (bolt-type axle) or an external threaded stud (nut-type axle). For some reason which no one has ever adequately been able to explain, the cranks are more likely to come loose from a nut-type axle than from a bolt type. If you are replacing an axle and have a choice of nut or bolt type, go for the bolt type every time.

Symptoms

Whatever type of bottom bracket you have, the symptoms of wear and maladjustment are much the same. Graunching or clicking noises from the crank area while pedalling, and cranks that can be rocked slightly from side to side (at right angles to their normal direction of movement) are usually indications of a loose, or worn bottom bracket.

If the cranks will not spin freely, then the bottom bracket is too tight. To check for this, drop the chain off the inside of the chainrings and spin the cranks. It'll be readily apparent if the bottom bracket is stiff; the cranks should spin freely, and they won't, they'll slow down after a couple of revolutions or less. If you have any of these problems in a Shimano, SunTour, FAG or Tioga cartridge bottom bracket, then it'll need replacing. The FAG and Shimano units need special tools, which any good bike shop will have. The Tioga unit is removed with standard bottom bracket tools and SunTour's also needs special tools, though it is unlikely you'll ever come across any but a Shimano unit on a production bike.

If the bottom bracket is not loose then a clicking noise could be due to a slightly loose crank, which should be tightened up as explained below, or a loose chainring or a loose pedal axle or pedal cage. See Chapter 12 for more on servicing pedals.

Tools

Unlike many parts of the bike, which can be fixed with just screwdrivers, spanners and Allen keys, bottom brackets do require special tools to dismantle and reassemble them properly. The minimum you'll need for a Shimano cartridge bottom bracket is a crank extractor and the Shimano tool for removing and fitting the cartridge unit. For a cup and cone bottom bracket you'll need your crank extractor, a lockring spanner and adjustable cup spanner. To remove the right-hand fixed cup you'll also need a fixed cup spanner, though this can be worked on in situ.

Madison Cycles do inexpensive versions of these tools, including adjustable ones for odd-sized cups and lockrings. A set of these is relatively cheap, but fine for home use. At the other end of the scale are Campagnolo, Park or Shimano tools — these will set you back a great deal more, but being pro quality and lasting forever they are worth considering for a club workshop. They also fit Sugino and SunTour bottom brackets. Somewhere in between in price are Tacx tools, which are good personal workshop units.

Probably the most important thing to remember about good, specialist bike tools like these is never lend them to anyone. By all means let other people use them, but good bike tools have a habit of never being seen again if you loan them out, which is what happened to my last set of Tacx bottom bracket tools.

Removing the cranks

The first thing you'll need to do to service an errant bottom bracket is to remove the cranks to get at the bottom bracket cups. We'll deal first with the simplest job, removing and replacing a Shimano cartridge bottom bracket, then go into the guts of a standard cup and cone bottom bracket. The first couple of steps are common to both.

If the dustcap is seized

Its not unknown for the dustcap to seize in the crank threads, and if this happens there are a number of ways of liberating it, though the more extreme methods require specialist

First, take the dust caps out of the cranks. Some can just be popped out with a screwdriver, some unscrew with a 5mm Allen key, others have a slot and can be unscrewed with a coin, and some have two little holes and can be unscrewed with needle nose pliers, or half a spoke, bent over to fit. Some 1993 and 1994 Shimano cranks attach by means of an 8mm Allen bolt; the dustcap is just a plastic ring which fits round the bolt and comes off with it. Dust caps are important for keeping the extractor threads in the crank arms clean — don't discard them

equipment, like a brazing torch. What usually happens is that the first attempt to remove the cap wrecks the slot or Allen keyhole, leaving you standing there feeling foolish and wondering what the hell to do next.

The first approach is always to drench the whole dustcap area in WD-40 or Duckoil, leave it for a few hours to work its way into the thread, then try to shift the cap. If there's anything left of the original Allen keyhole a screwdriver blade of the right size can sometimes be forced in to turn the cap. Options include, cutting a slot in the cap with a saw if there is enough of the cap standing proud of the crank, (don't cut the crank!), drilling holes in the

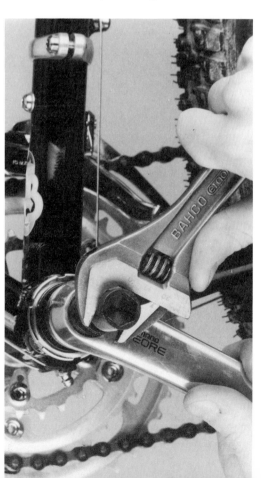

Bottom left:
The crank is held on with a 14mm bolt and washer or a nut, or with an 8mm Allen bolt in the case of many 1993 Shimano cranks, and almost all 1994 Shimano cranks

Bottom right:
with the extractor fitted in the crank, use a spanner to turn the extractor punch and drive the crank off the axle

cap and turning it with needle nosed pliers, and drilling down the thread to break the cap.

As a last resort plastic dustcaps can be burnt out with a brazing torch. All of these are a pro mechanic's desperate measures and should not be attempted by novices who might easily do more damage than good. If replacing dustcaps, fit plastic ones; they're light, do the job and are easy to force out if necessary.

Most crank extractors have a socket in one end to remove 14mm bolts and nuts use it with a medium-sized adjustable spanner to remove the bolt or nut. If you have TA cranks (now very unlikely, but some early MTBs used them) or Campagnolo cranks, they use 15mm bolts and need either the special 15mm socket spanner these companies make to remove them, or a very thin-walled standard socket. All others are 15mm. Remember to take the washer out with the bolt. Problems like this are less likely if you use the same brand of extractor as your cranks and keep the crank threads clean. To remove the crank, turn the inner part of the extractor clockwise so that it pushes on the axle and pulls the crank off the thread. Repeat for the other crank.

Brute force crank removal

If the extractor threads in the crank are damaged, or the end of the crank has become damaged, preventing the extractor from going in, you'll need to resort to rather more extreme methods of getting the crank off.

VAR make a special tool which grabs the crank and pushes against the axle to get it off, but like most methods of removing a damaged crank it tends to write it off by bending it. If you're going to tackle removing a stripped crank, be prepared to replace it afterwards.

The simplest method of removing a striped crank is to take the bolt out and hit the back of the crank, using a hammer and a 12-inch long piece of 1/2inch steel bar as a drift. Hit just next to the axle. Eventually the crank will fly across the room. Make sure there's no one in the way!

A subtler technique is to use an automotive gear puller, which has two arms to grip the back of the crank, and a pusher which pushes against the axle. This can be difficult to use on right-hand cranks, since it is awkward to get the arms evenly spaced; the five-arm spider gets in the way.

With both of these techniques there is a chance of getting the crank off intact, though I wouldn't want to have a stripped crank lying round the place — someone might try to use it. The last method destroys the square taper, but has the advantage of needing no special tools. Just take off the crank bolt and continue to ride the bike. Sooner or later the crank will work loose and drop off. Make sure you have a spare to hand.

Removing the bottom bracket
Shimano cartridge

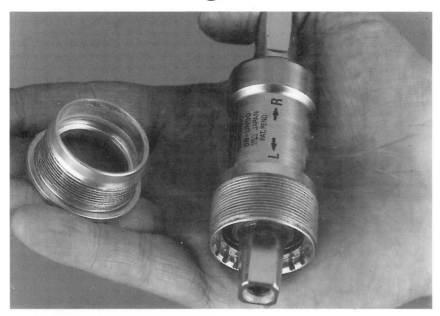

This is a Shimano cartridge bottom bracket, in this case a BB-UN90 XTR model from a rather nice Cannondale Super V full suspension bike. It consists of a lump which houses the axle and bearings, and screws into one side of the frame, and a locking collar which screws into the other side, shown in the frame in the first picture

Both sides unscrew by means of a special splined Shimano tool. The drive side is left-hand threaded and therefore unscrews clockwise, the other side is a standard right-hand thread

Cup and cone bottom bracket

To remove a cup and cone bottom bracket, first unscrew the lockring on the non-drive side. This has a right-hand thread and therefore unscrews anti clockwise. It should be in tight; don't be afraid to be forceful with it. This Park spanner has just one tooth to engage the ring; some, like Shimano's and Campagnolo's, have more, and are better at shifting stubborn or slightly corroded bottom brackets

Unscrew the fixed cup with a peg spanner. If the bottom bracket cups are in good condition and were greased on original assembly it will come out easily, but it's not unusual to find that a bit of oomph is needed to get it moving. Take the cup and bearings out of the frame

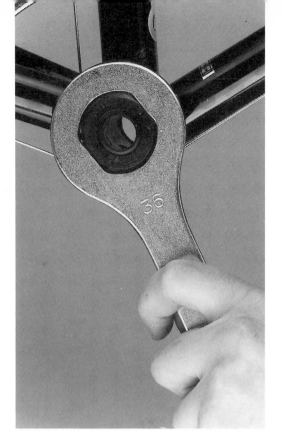

Pull the axle out of the bottom bracket, and if there is a removable sleeve in there, pull that out too. Put the axle and fixed cup to one side. Clean the cups, axle and bearings thoroughly with solvent

The fixed cup is left-hand threaded and therefore unscrews clockwise. It can be cleaned in situ with a rag and solvent, but its easier to get at if you remove it, and if you want to inspect the bearing surface for wear, which, ideally, you do, then it will have to come out

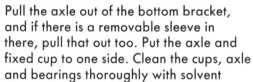

It can be difficult to get all the old grease out of caged bearings like those shown, so we advocate chucking them away and replacing them with loose balls

The only parts that are the same for virtually all bottom brackets are the bearing balls, which are quarter-inch in size and 22 in number (11 per side). Make sure you get proper industrial quality bearings such as RHP or FAG, not steel balls which are about as round as cake decorations, but not as tasty.

In general it's better to replace caged balls in a cup and cone bottom bracket with loose ones, for a bunch of reasons. Widely available caged balls are generally of poor quality; loose balls are easier to clean and service and you can get more balls into the same space (11 instead of the nine usually found in cages) spreading the load and prolonging the life of all the components of the bottom bracket. In theory caged balls reduce ball to ball friction, and the ideal system would be a cage with 11 balls, these do exist but are rare. In practice this is a minor consideration; getting dirty grease out of a caged bearing is so much hassle that it negates any other advantages.

Worthy of mention at this point is SunTour's and Wilderness Trail Bike's Grease Guard system, which uses special bearings with built-in grease ports and a fine-nozzle grease injector to allow the user to pump fresh grease into the bottom bracket, and also the pedals, headset and hub bearings.

Grease Guard components work superbly, as long as you remember to change the grease in them pretty often. Don't neglect them, though. In order to let the grease out, they are not as well sealed as some bearings

Inspect the bearing surfaces and balls for signs of wear. A smooth track (top) where the balls run on the axle or in the cup, is fine, but any bearing surface which shows signs of pitting should be replaced; a pitted axle usually means a pitted cup too, and you'll need to replace the whole lot

(they don't need to be, you're supposed to clean them after every wet ride) and so they will let water in and get corroded if you don't keep up with greasing them. For diligent riders, they are ideal.

Replacing the bottom bracket

When you go to the bike shop to get new parts for your bottom bracket, take the old ones with you. Even if you're just getting a new Shimano cartridge unit, lengths and shell sizes do differ, and its much easier for the shop's salesperson or mechanic to find you the right replacement part if they've got the original to work from, rather than a vague description.

Installing a bottom bracket

Before installing the bottom bracket, clean out the inside of the bottom bracket shell in the frame with solvent and a rag, to prevent the new, or newly cleaned, pieces from picking up old dirt and crud.

Fit the fixed cup into the drive side of the frame. This is exactly the opposite of removing it. Remember that it's a left-hand thread; it screws in anticlockwise

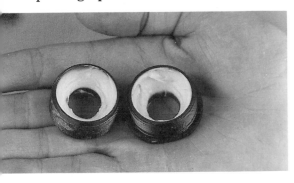

Smear lots of fresh, clean grease in the cups

To prevent corrosion, and make the cup easy to remove, smear a little grease on the thread before fitting it, especially if you are fitting a steel cup into an aluminium frame or vice versa. It should be possible to screw in the fixed cup most of the way by hand or with just very light force from a spanner. If it is very stiff it may be cross-threaded or the threads may need a clearing tap running through them, a job for a bike shop.

Place the bearings in the grease, 11 per side, then add more grease over the top of them to stick them in place. We don't believe it is possible to have too much grease in a bottom bracket

If you screw a cross-threaded cup into a frame you may do very expensive damage, so proceed cautiously. Finally, tighten the cup down hard. It should be as tight as possible to prevent it coming loose under pedalling loads.

Put the sleeve, if there is one, into the bottom bracket shell, then put the axle through into the fixed cup from the other side. Most axles are asymmetrical; the longer side goes on the drive side to accommodate the greater thickness of the chainrings. Take care not to dislodge any balls when fitting the axle.

Grease the fixed cup thread and screw it into the frame until it stops against the axle. Fit the lockring on to the cup and adjust the cup so that the axle turns smoothly with no play. Tighten the lockring while holding the cup in place with the peg spanner. Check the axle for play.

Replacing the cranks

Clean the ends of the axle with solvent, and clean out the inside of the crank arms as well. Cranks should be mounted on the axle dry, they are practically the only aluminium to steel joint on the bike which is like this, and the reason is that the square taper fit they use relies on the metal-metal friction to stop the crank from going on too far. A greasy crank slides further than it is intended to on to the axle, and this can overstress and thus weaken the crank

Usually, tightening the lockring pulls the cup out of the frame slightly and produces a small amount of bearing play. If this has happened, loosen the lockring and adjust the cup so that the bearing is very slightly stiff (initially, over-tighten the bearing a little) then tighten the lockring. You may need to repeat this a few times to get it spot on.

If you are at all unsure of how to carry on, at any stage in the reassembling of a bottom bracket, ask your friendly neighbourhood bike shop. We once had a very irate customer return to the shop with a wrecked bottom bracket. He'd forced the cups into the wrong sides of the frame and, just for good measure, screwed the pedals into the wrong cranks. All new equipment, all expensively ruined, and, he claimed, all our fault because we hadn't told him how to fit it. Since he hadn't asked, we'd assumed he knew what he was doing. If you interrogated everyone who buys anything on a busy Saturday about their level of mechanical knowledge you'd soon go bust! If in doubt, ask.

If you've got threaded dustcaps,

Slide the cranks on to the axle, then grease the crank bolts and screw them into the cranks. Remember to put the cranks at 180° to each other. (You may well laugh, but I've seen experienced mechanics jump on to hastily assembled bikes only to find the cranks at 90°)

Tighten the crank bolts down hard; limit of strength with an eight-inch adjustable spanner is about right for most people

grease them. A seized steel dustcap is a first class pain to remove. We prefer plastic dustcaps which are self-lubricating and can be melted out if necessary. A more expensive but more practical option are Allen key crank removers like Shimano's old One-Key Releases, Sugino's Autex devices, Syncros' Crank-o-Matics and Zero Components' Zippies. As the name suggests Allen key crank removers allow the cranks to be removed with just the Allen key and fit in place of the dustcaps.

Chainrings

There was a time when chainrings on mountain bikes was a simple subject. Everyone, but everyone, made rings that used the same bolt circle diameters. This is the size of the circle in which the five fixing bolts which attach a ring to a crank are arranged. Outer and middle rings used to have a 110mm bolt circle diameter and the inner ring was 74mm. SunTour's introduction of Micro Drive in 1992 changed all that.

A Micro Drive system has smaller chainrings and sprockets, to produce the same range of gears as a conventional system, but with less material and therefore lower weight, and uses bolt circle diameters of 94mm and 56mm.

For 1994 Shimano have announced their version, Hyperdrive-C (for compact) which uses a combination of rings with special steel ramps to speed up shifting (the Hyperdrive part of the name) and Micro Drive-

style small rings. Unfortunately Shimano have chosen to use a different bolt circle from SunTour for their inner rings (58mm) and a different standard for cheaper groups than for expensive ones.

Groups at and below STX level in Shimano's 1994 line-up have 95mm bolt circles, Deore XT and the two versions of Deore LX have a 94mm spec.

At the time of writing, however, all of this is gleaned from Shimano's 1994 manufacturer's handbook. It is possible that by the time this equipment sees production, things may have changed. In any case the practical upshot of all this is that you should take the old parts to the shop with you if replacing worn Hyperdrive-C rings.

Worn chainrings

Chainrings wear out. No surprise, really, since they are usually made from aluminium alloy while chains are made from hardened steel. The usual symptom of a worn chainring is the chain slipping in all the gears, but only on one ring, and usually the middle chainring goes first because it is the most used. The solution is to replace it.

Outer and middle rings are easy to remove with the crank still on the bike, but to get at the inner ring you'll need to take the right-hand crank arm off the axle as described above.

The rings are held on by 5mm Allen keys of a design which is unique to chainsets. The inner ring has five bolts which screw directly into the inside of the crank arms and the middle and outer rings are linked by nut-and-bolt pairs that go through the ends of the crank spider arms. Unscrew all the necessary nuts and bolts and put them somewhere safe

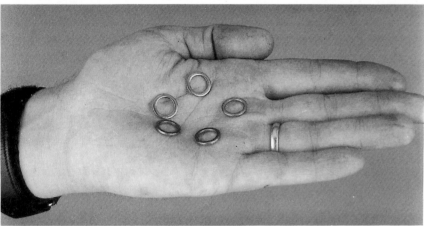

If there are any washers or spacers, make a note of where they go (usually between the middle ring and the crank spider) and keep them with the bolts

A 110mm outer ring is usually big enough to pass comfortably over the pedal, and the middle ring will usually fit with a bit of fiddling, though if you have large pedals you may need to take the pedal off. To do this you need a 15mm pedal spanner. Unscrew the pedal anticlockwise. Removing Micro Drive-style rings will almost certainly oblige you to take off the pedal

Chainring replacement

There is a wide variety of replacement chainrings available, and the main differences between them are in the quality of the materials used to make them and in the way in which they are shaped or designed to aid shifting.

The first difference is between aluminium alloy and stainless steel. Aluminium has been the material of choice for years because it is light, but there are several different grades of the material which are suitable for shaping into rings. It is worth spending the extra money on rings made from harder grade aluminium, such as those from Pace, SR, Mavic, Campagnolo and Shimano's XTR and Deore XT rings. Very small rings tend to wear out quickly if made from aluminium, so several manufacturers have introduced steel inner rings in the last couple of years. Onza

Buzzsaws and SR Ninja rings are well known, but Shimano also make steel inner rings.

A recent complication is the introduction of shaped ramps and guides on chainrings to aid shifting. Shimano's Superdrive and Hyperdrive rings, and Sugino's Supershift rings have this feature, and all shift better than standard flat rings. However, if you have one of these systems you need to get the right replacement parts to keep it working well, and spares availability has been patchy up to now. We have seen spare XTR Hyperdrive rings, though, so persist in getting your dealer to hassle the Shimano spares office if you need them. Many dealers seem to take the attitude that Shimano spares are simply unavailable and don't bother to try.

Where possible, replace Shimano outer and middle rings with XTR or Deore XT parts. The extra cost is worth it for the increased durability. If you have a 1993 Shimano chainset, replace the inner ring with a 24-toother, rather than the too-big 26er that Shimano inexplicably fitted to all their 1993 chainsets. If you have a 1994 STX or Alivio chainset, then you're out of luck; you won't be able to replace the rings with anything better than STX quality. We can only conclude that this is deliberate, and the reason why there is a 1mm difference between the high-end and low-end cranks bolt circles is to force people to buy an entire new chainset to get better quality rings.

All special rings (Hyperdrive, Supershift, the old elliptical Biopace, and so on) have tabs on the rings which align with the crank arm so that they shift properly, or, in the case of Biopace, correctly provide the biomechanical advantages claimed for them

8: HUBS AND FREEWHEELS

Hubs perch in the middle of the wheel, like a couple of alloy spiders in a stainless steel web, usually forgotten until something goes wrong with them. This isn't often if you keep them clean and well-maintained, but will be if you tend to ride through rivers and neglect them. Like those of bottom brackets, hub bearings come in two main variants, lip-sealed cup-and-cone (standard) bearing type and sealed cartridge bearing.

The latter have fallen out of favour in recent years and it is very unusual to find them as original equipment on a production bike. To improve standard bearing hubs Shimano introduced the freehub in 1988, a system where the freewheel was effectively part of the hub, rather than a separate unit which screwed onto it. This allowed them to space the rear hub bearings further apart, better supporting the rear axle and effectively strengthening it.

Another advantage of freehubs is that the sprockets simply slide onto splines on the freewheel mechanism. Shimano hold their sprockets on with a lockring, SunTour use a screw-on top sprocket. This makes changes of sprockets relatively cheap and easy. Because Hyperglide's incredibly fast and smooth shifts rely on precise alignment of the pickup teeth and release teeth on adjacent sprockets it is essential that they are aligned properly, and so the sprockets have one spline which is larger than the others to force correct fitting. The SunTour/WTB Greaseguard system on the top-line XC-Pro group looked as though it might make cartridge bearing hubs popular again, but the very late availability of these components in 1990, followed by the hopelessness of early samples of SunTour's Micro Drive equipment meant that this didn't happen and probably now won't.

Signs of wear and maladjustment are similar to other bearings. If the hubs are too tight or worn the axle will not turn smoothly in the hub; if they are too loose the wheel will rattle slightly in the frame. Grab the tyre and try and move it from side to side. If it moves at all, attention is needed. An over-tight hub may not be obvious while the wheel is still in the frame, so it's worth taking the wheels out occasionally to check the bearings.

The other things that go wrong with hubs have to do with the freewheel mechanism and the sprockets mounted on it. There is usually no need to do more than keep these clean until they become so worn that one or all of them needs replacing. You usually find out that this is necessary when you've just fitted a new chain and the transmission still slips because the sprocket teeth have become slightly worn. Its rare to find that all the sprockets are worn – usually just the smaller ones, or the couple you use most will be shot.

To get the sprockets off you will need a pair of chain whips, or, for Shimano Hyperglide systems, a chain whip and a Hyperglide lockring tool (TL HG 15). The internals of the freehub, or of an old-style screw-on freewheel, have got to be the least user-serviceable parts of a bike and our general advice is leave well alone.

Regular flushing with a light spray oil such as Superspray Lube or Cyclon Course will clean out the bearings and a follow-through with a heavier oil such as Cyclon MTB will keep them turning. The place to spray lubricant is the tiny gap between the outer part of the freewheel body, which moves, and the inner part, which doesn't. If a freewheel or freehub is still excessively graunchy, or sticks, or freewheels in both directions, and lubrication doesn't cure the problem, then frankly it is simpler to replace it than to service it.

The guts of Shimano freehub bodies are now simpler today, but replacement ones can be had from Shimano, and it's so much easier to just slap a new one on that it hardly seems worth trying to dismantle and service them.

Shimano freehub bodies are removed and replaced with a 10mm Allen key which fits down the inside of the hub when the axle has been removed. A removing tool exists for Dura-Ace freehubs, but it will not work on any mountain bike freehub; you need a 10mm Allen key.

Cheaper SunTour equipped bikes still use screw-on freewheels. Again these can be serviced, in theory, but in practice it's not worth the hassle since new ones aren't expensive. More expensive SunTour groupsets have SunTour's freehub design, which has a steel sleeve that goes right through the hub to retain the freehub body, avoiding the use of a steel bolt in a fine aluminium thread, which SunTour feel is the main disadvantage of the Shimano system. This is removed with a 10mm Allen key.

For general servicing of hubs, a set of thin cone spanners is one of the best investments you can make. Campagnolos are the best and still quite reasonably priced. You'll need a set that consists of a pair of 13mm/14mm double ended cone spanners, a pair of 15/16mm units and standard 15mm, 16mm or 17mm spanners to fit the lock-nuts. The last three vary from hub to hub so take your bike with you when buying tools or use a good quality adjustable spanner. It's cheaper to use Bicycle Research spanners which have jaws that double up; the outer portion of each jaw is, say, 14mm and the inner is 13mm, with a 15/16mm pairing in the other end. You'll need two of these.

Using a quick release

This may seem like an elementary skill to more experienced riders, but we do occasionally see rookie riders who don't know how to use their QRs properly. Here's how a wheel quick release works.

A quick release is a cam-action device which holds the wheel into the dropout. The lever moves towards the wheel and as it does so it tightens the cap against the dropout. A well-designed quick release is actually more secure than a nut, because the cam backs off the force on the dropout very slightly in the last few degrees of its movement. This means for it to spontaneously open that force has to increase, which is impossible.

To open a QR, pull the lever away from the wheel. Don't try to rotate it; it's not a big nut

A fully open QR. The wheel should now just fall out of the dropout. However, most forks have dropouts with lips which prevent this, which has the effect of turning the quick release into a slow release. We file them off the forks on our bikes

This is what a properly closed quick release should look like. The handle should curve toward the wheel and the word *close* should be visible on the handle

To adjust the amount of force necessary to open and close the QR, turn the nut on the other side of the wheel while holding the QR lever. The lever should start to need distinct effort to move it about halfway round its movement, that is, when it is sticking straight out from the wheel, and should leave a dent in your palm when fully closed

Servicing the hub

We deal here with a complete strip-down and re-build of a Shimano Hyperglide rear hub, since this covers most of the problems you might come across and is far and away the most common type. A front hub is simpler in construction, but the basic principles are the same. As far as dismantling goes, you'll usually need 13mm cone spanners to take a front hub apart.

Dismantling the rear hub

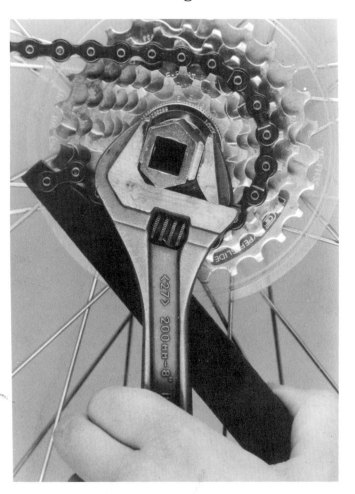

Start by removing the sprocket cluster, or cassette, from the hub. Strictly speaking, this isn't absolutely necessary, but it gets what is usually a large and grubby item out of the way. Hyperglide sprockets, and the sprockets on SunTour's freehubs slide on to splines on the freehub body.

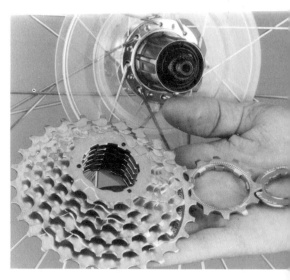

Lift the lockring, outer sprocket, washer and cassette off the freehub body. Put them somewhere safe. If you are working on a front hub, you can ignore this and the first step, of course

Left: Shimano sprockets are held on by a lockring, SunTour ones by a threaded top sprocket, which will need a pair of chain whips to remove it.
  Take out the skewer by unscrewing the nut on the end and catching the spring as it falls off. Then take off the lockring which retains the sprockets with a Shimano TL HG-15 tool and a chain whip

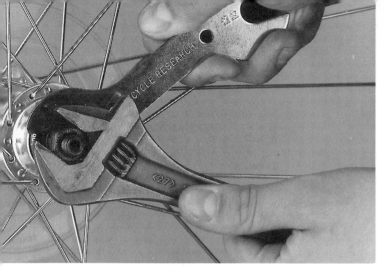

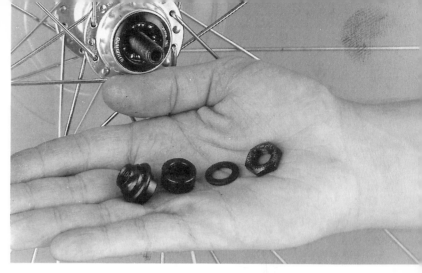

Turn the wheel over, and undo the locknut on the non-drive side of the axle. Hold the cone with a thin cone spanner (usually 15mm for a rear hub, 13mm for front) and unscrew the locknut with a fixed spanner (sizes vary between hubs) or good adjustable. If the cone is a tight fit it may be necessary to hold the lock-nut on the other end of the axle with a spanner while you unscrew it, but cones can usually be unscrewed by hand

Remove the locknut, any spacers and washers, and the cone. This is a typical set of bits from an axle, but don't fret if yours don't look exactly like this, they do vary. Make a note of the order in which all these bits came off the hub. Take care not to lose the washer, especially if it has a tab; replacements are notoriously hard to find

Lift the axle out of the hub, taking care not to dislodge the bearings, though the plastic dustcaps in most hubs will prevent them from falling out. Clean the cones with solvent and inspect them for damage. Any sign of pitting on a cone indicates that it should be replaced, along with the bearings and is usually a sign that the bearing race in the hub will be damaged as well

Carefully prise out the dustcap, working round it gently to avoid damage. A damaged dustcap is worse than useless, so go easy at this stage

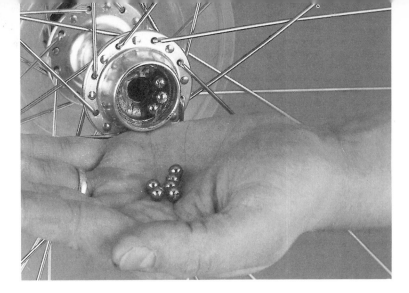

Drop the bearings out. Clean them and check for signs of pitting. Replace the whole set if any of the balls are damaged

The bearings in a front hub are 3/16inch size, and there are nine per side. Rear hub bearings are slightly larger, 1/4inch, and there are also nine per side. There are rare exceptions, however, so take one of the old ones along when buying replacements. Its sensible to buy a few more than this because they do tend to run away across the workshop floor and hide under large, heavy objects. (The strongest force in the universe is Fridge Suck, the attraction the space under any white household object exerts on a ball bearing.)

With the hub shell bare you can now clean the bearing surfaces of the cup and inspect them for wear. A smoothly worn bearing track is acceptable, but any sign of pitting indicates that they should be replaced. Unfortunately, replacement cup bearing surfaces are only available for Campag hubs and this is why it is vitally important to maintain them.

Since most hubs, especially Shimano freehubs, are only available as pairs, a single worn cup can land you with a hefty bill for replacement hubs and

wheel-building. If the bearing surface in the freehub body is damaged, then you'll have to replace the whole body, but not the hub.

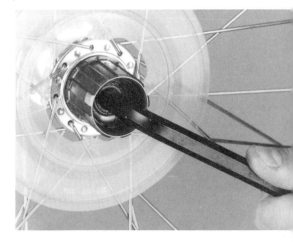

The freehub body is held in place with a hollow nut that takes a 10mm Allen key

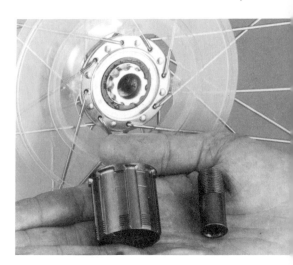

The freehub body lifts off as a complete unit. Replace the whole body if the old one has become unacceptably worn. To refit it, grease the bolt and screw it in firmly. SunTour freehubs use a similar system, but the 10mm bolt screws in from the other side of the hub and threads into the freehub body centre

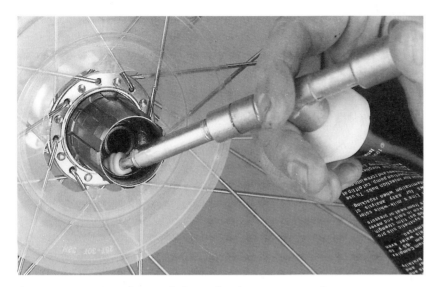

Smear a generous layer of clean, fresh grease into the bearing surfaces, enough to hold the bearings in place as you reassemble the hub. Wash your hands first to prevent dirt contaminating the grease

Place the clean or new bearings in the grease. Don't be tempted to squeeze in more than nine per side even if there seems to be room

Push the dustcaps back in using firm finger pressure. A further gentle tap from a rubber mallet might be needed just to finally seat them into place

Before you put the axle back in, make sure the drive side locknut and cone are very tight against each other. For some reason, it always seems to be this side that comes apart. We're assured by people who have an understanding of the more arcane aspects of bearing science that there is a good reason for this, and it's not just the natural cussedness of inanimate objects.

Since this bearing is hard to get at to adjust when the hub is fully assembled, it's worth making sure it's damn tight.

Then replace the axle, put the cone, spacer(s) and locknuts back on, adjust the bearing and tighten the locknut, while holding the cone with a cone spanner. The bearings should turn smoothly and freely with no play.

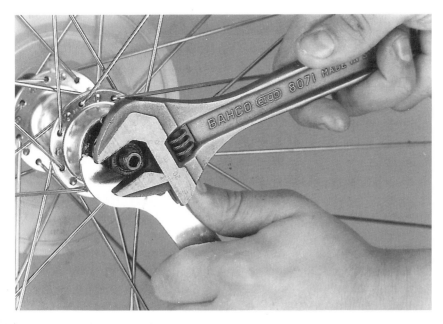

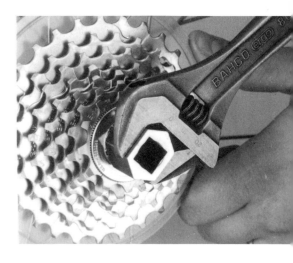

Top right: put the axle back in, screw on the cone, fit the washer and locknut, adjust the bearing then tighten the locknut firmly while holding the cone with a cone spanner

Tighten the lockring with the TL HG15 tool. If the tool pops out of the splines before the lockring is tight enough, put the quick release skewer through the whole lot to hold it together. Make sure the lockring is well tight. A loose lockring in the middle of nowhere is a major problem, and you can bet your TL HG 15 will be at home

Slide in the cassette, making sure to align the large spline (it won't go on otherwise!). Fit the washer, top sprocket and lockring

Screw-on freewheels

Servicing some older rear hubs is complicated by the presence of a freewheel. A conventional screw-on freewheel must be removed before the cones can be adjusted. This is done with a freewheel remover, a tool which fits in or on to the centre of the freewheel, and turns just the inner body without involving the freewheel mechanism. (If you tried to unscrew a freewheel by turning the sprockets it would just free-wheel.)

Different freewheels need different tools to remove them, so again, take your bike along to the shop with you.

The most common type are probably the Shimano Uniglide and Hyperglide, which take a splined remover, and SunTour's Accushift freewheel which takes a four-pronged tool. Do not attempt to remove a SunTour four-pronged freewheel with a two-pronged tool — this fits the old Perfect and New Winner models — because either the tool or the prongs on the freewheel may break, making it next to impossible to remove.

As an aside to all this, if you are cutting the spokes to take the rim off a wheel in order to have it rebuilt, remove the freewheel first. A hub and freewheel are all but impossible to separate once the wheel has been cut apart. This is not a problem with freehubs.

To remove the freewheel, place the tool in the freewheel body and hold it in place with the quick release skewer or nut. Clamp the tool in a vice and twist the whole wheel anticlockwise until it starts to turn. With the freewheel thus loosened you can now remove the wheel from the vice, loosen the quick release or axle nut and unscrew the freewheel. If you haven't got a vice, a large adjustable spanner will usually provide enough leverage to shift the freewheel, though you may need to enlist the help of another pair of arms. Once you've got the freewheel off, servicing is the same as for a front hub. Smear grease on the freewheel thread, when replacing it, to stop it seizing up.

To remove the sprockets from a conventional freewheel, first wrap a chain whip around a sprocket in the middle of the block so that it pulls the freewheel clockwise. Wrap the other chain whip around the top sprocket so it pulls anticlockwise. Position the two chain whips so that the handles cross and you can undo the top sprocket by squeezing them together with both hands. This may require a considerable amount of force, especially if the cluster has been used for a long time, which is why the mechanic mentioned in Chapter two ended up with a home-made set of Armageddon chain whips for shifting stubborn top sprockets.

Another reason why you might want to change sprockets is to change the gearing of your mountain bike. We run the standard 12-28 cluster for racing and fun riding, but switch to a 13-30 or 14-32 for touring, and Shimano even make a 13-34 that provides ultra-low gearing for heavily laden, steep tours. You are restricted to the standard clusters Shimano offer if you want to run Hyperglide, but SunTour and non-Hyperglide Shimano systems allow you to mix and match sprockets to create custom gear systems.

How gears work

To understand gears, you need to know how to calculate a gear ratio, and the way these are quoted is a bit odd. We talk about gears in inches, but this number is not, as you might expect, the distance along the ground that one turn of the pedals would take you. To find out what it means we have to take a short trip back to the 1870s when Ordinary or penny farthing bikes were used.

These early machines had a large front wheel which was driven directly by the pedals without chains or gears. The larger the front wheel the faster you could go for a given pedalling speed, which is why they got so big in the first place. The gear of one of these bikes was expressed in terms of the size of the wheel, and when chain driven bikes began to appear the manufacturers quoted their gear sizes in terms of the size of wheel an Ordinary would need, to have the same gear. It's archaic, but the system has survived to this day.

On the Continent they have a much more sensible system; they quote the development, which is the distance in metres that the bike travels for one turn of the pedals.

To work out a gear ratio, divide the number of teeth on the chainwheel (C) by the number on the rear sprocket (S) and multiply by the size of the rear wheel, in inches (W). Or, $G = (C/S) \times W$

For a mountain bike W is almost always 26 inches, though some smaller bikes have 24inch wheels. The size will be marked on the side of the tyre. A typical gear set of 24, 36, and 46 teeth chainrings and a 12-28 cluster has a range from 22 inches to 100 inches. The lowest gear is produced by the 24/28 combination, and the highest by the 46/12. At a comfortable pedalling rate of 80 rpm these produce speeds of 24mph and 5mph, respectively.

To go faster or slower on a bike with this set-up you change your pedalling speed, though one of the reasons why bikes have gears is that human beings are only efficient within a fairly narrow range of pedalling rates, so if you find yourself climbing at under 3mph you'd be more efficient if you got off and walked, or fitted a lower bottom gear. Extreme gear systems are useful for some unusual applications. I know one tinkerer who runs a 14inch gear, achieved by using a modified 18-tooth sprocket as a chainring and running it through a 32-tooth rear sprocket. This gear allows him to climb ridiculously steep slopes, but he needs very good balance to stay on at under 2mph.

At the other end of the scale, downhill racers like World Champion Greg Herbold run enormous 62/12 combinations on the steep, smooth descents of California's notorious Kamikaze run at Mammoth Mountain.

Cartridge bearing hubs

Cartridge bearings are complete sealed assemblies containing a cone, a cup, several ball bearings and a small quantity of grease. Unfortunately, because these bearings are designed to be sealed for life, there's little a home mechanic can do to service them. Removing the bearings would cause damage to their outer races, so any lubrication has to be done in situ. The only maintenance you can do yourself is periodic regreasing by removing the outer rubber seals and smearing grease into the bearing. Thankfully damaged bearings are reasonably easy to replace, and as there is no wear on the axle or hub, with occasional bearing replacement a hub will last you a long time.

To replace the bearings in SunTour XC-Comp and XC-Pro cartridge bearing hubs first get replacements from a SunTour dealer, who can obtain them from the importer, along with the necessary tools to fit them. Take the lock-nuts, washers and bearing mountings (the bits where the cones would be on a cup and cone hub) off the axle and, if this leaves one end in a bearing, tap it out with a rubber hammer. If you have to use a conventional hammer, put a nut over the end of the axle to prevent damage to the threads.

This leaves the bearings in the shell. Tap the old ones out with the SunTour tool and a length of steel bar (a drift). This of course destroys the bearings since the force needed to separate the bearing body from the shell is transmitted through the bearings, knocking dents into the balls and surfaces. However, since the reason you're taking the old bearings out is because they've had it anyway, this doesn't matter.

To fit the new bearings use the special thick washers SunTour supply to push them in by the outer race only. This prevents you doing the kind of damage we've just mentioned. Fit a washer and bearing over the bearing mounting on the axle and put the other bearing, washer and mounting on the axle. Screw the bearing mounts together until the bearings have been pushed all the way into the hub shell.

Routine maintenance

I like to wipe a little grease on the exposed steel parts of my hubs, just to stop them rusting, but otherwise there's not much you can do in the way of day-to-day hub maintenance except service them as soon as they develop a problem. One modification I have seen on a few standard hubs is the fitting of a grease nipple in the middle of the hub shell, so that fresh grease can be easily pumped into the bearings, especially after they've been immersed. This is easiest to do on brand-new hubs, or when you're having your wheels rebuilt, and is the kind of a job an engineering-inclined mechanic should be able to do for you fairly easily.

9: WHEELS

Wheel builders are often referred to as mechanics with a mystical mechanical aptitude that gives them an uncanny knack of mending bicycles simply by laying their hands on them. Well, it's kind-of true: to learn how to build strong wheels takes quite some time, and is definitely best learned with a skilled wheelbuilder alongside you to give you some pointers. Wheel trueing, the art of fixing a wobbly wheel, is easier. First you need to understand how a wheel stays together (or doesn't).

A bicycle wheel is an excellently designed engineering structure, consisting of individually weak component parts that come together to form a super strong structure. Spokes (thin wire lengths) support the rim (a rolled aluminium alloy extrusion) and connect it to the hub. Wheels gain their strength from the properties of the spokes and the rim. A wheel's beauty is that the spokes are allowed to flex to dissipate shock and disperse the impact throughout the wheel. A rim is stiff to allow the dispersion of stress over as many spokes as possible. All in all it is a remarkable engineering creation having a strength to weight ratio in excess of 500:1.

Let's take a more in depth look at the various parts, before we see how to maintain them.

Rims

A box section rim

A twin channel rim

Rims are formed by forcing hot aluminium alloy through a die to give a long length of aluminium bar with the right cross-section as the finished rim needs. Lengths of this extrusion are then rolled and joined to form a hoop. How they're joined is reasonably academic: welding, bonding and riveting are all used at the moment, and none seems to be significantly better than the other. None affect the braking capacity of the bike. By the time the sidewalls of the rim are covered in mud and grit, the joint of the rim is the least of your worries when it comes to braking. The rim is then drilled to take the spokes, and eyelets may be fitted. These are small brass bushes which act as ferrules, spreading the load from the spoke away from the hole in the rim. Some rims have them, and they're heavier than not having them (obviously); some builders love 'em, some don't.

When designing a rim, the designer can choose where to put the metal in the cross-section. Lighter designs need better quality alloys to maintain the correct strength, and better alloys are usually harder to extrude. More complicated cross-sections require more expensive dies. All this means that there are many different types of rim, varying from the awful to the awfully good. In a recent test I conducted for *MBUK*, FIR rims proved the best, followed by Mavic and Campagnolo. A rim from these manufacturers won't go far wrong for you.

Spokes

These are lengths of rolled steel, formed with a bend at one end, and a thread rolled at the other for the nipple to screw onto. They come in hundreds of different lengths and different cross-sections for different uses.

A spoke's thickness is measured by the confusing Standard Wire Gauge. Spokes have been getting lighter on mountain bikes over the past few years, as the revolving weight of the wheel is an important area to try and save weight. Early wheels were built with 36x14g spokes, around 2mm thick.

The spokes fitted to many entry level bikes are stainless steel with a uniform 'plain gauge' profile, but increasingly better bikes are coming with double or single butted spokes, with the end nearest the rim thinner than the end in the hub.

This double butting process thins the spoke's section in the centre, resulting in the diameter dropping from the 2mm at the ends, to 1.6mm. This might sound like a small change, but it can save quarter of a pound on a set of wheels. Also, the spoke's flexibility is increased, resulting in a stronger set of wheels. If you're having a set of wheels built, it's well worth asking for double butted spokes.

Spoke Nipples

Weight savings can be made here too. Previously all spoke nipples were chrome-plated brass, but aluminium alloy has become the vogue, saving another couple of ounces. Ultimately they're not as strong as brass nipples, but if you use them in a well-built set of wheels they'll be fine. They're not great in low-priced or production bike wheels which generally need more attention throughout their life. Aluminium nipples round off their

A rear wheel showing 2-cross lacing on the far side and radial spoking on the near side

A rear wheel showing 3-cross lacing

flats and make maintenance a hassle.

How a wheel works

The spoking pattern on a wheel means that the load is spread across many spokes instead of just one. The tension in these spokes keeps the wheel spinning in a circle — most of the time. When a wheel goes out of true it's because a spoke, or the rim, has been permanently bent. A wheel then is a tug of war match for the spokes on opposing sides of the hub. The harder they pull, the harder it is for you to knock the wheel out of shape . . . up to a point. If you exceed a certain tension, the wheel flips itself into a crisp shape, and wrecks the rim. It's this tension that is critical to gauge and is what makes wheelbuilding so tricky.

Truing a wheel

To true a wheel you don't need the full kit of wheel jigs and dishing tool, although if you do have them it really helps. A spoke key is really all that's needed, and you can use the brake blocks to check for alignment.

There are two sorts of misalign-ment that occur in a wheel: lateral or sideways bending, and vertical distortion resulting in a rim bobbing up and down when you spin it. It's best to deal with the corrections in that order, rather than try the other way, or deal with both at once. This again is where experience counts, as you can correct both problems with

Correcting lateral misalignment

Correcting vertical misalignment

one operation, but it takes skill and patience.

Find the section of the wheel that is knocked out of line sideways, and see which way it's bent. If there are several wobbles, work on the worst one first.

Let's say for our case that the wheel is bent to the left. Tighten the spoke, from the right side of the hub at the most damaged point, by half a turn. Loosen the two adjacent spokes at the rim on the left side of the hub

by a quarter turn, spin the wheel and see what has happened. If the rim is badly bent, tighten the adjacent spokes by a quarter turn on the right side. Check for the error in the rim, and if it's still there, repeat the process, but only tweaking the spokes another half or quarter turn at a time. The worst thing you can do is to haul the rim back to the right position by putting five turns into one spoke, instead of distributing the correction across several spokes.

If you've now got the wheel running so that it doesn't wobble from side to side, check it doesn't jump up and down. This happens when it's deformed so that it is no longer truly circular. At a high point, tighten the spokes half a turn on both sides of the rim, whereas if the rim bobs downwards, slacken the spokes by half a turn at that point. This may have affected the side-to-side wobble again, so go back and check it. Getting a wheel accurately circular again takes time and patience and the only way is to do small amounts of correction several times to get the wheel back to normal. Sometimes a rim may be too

A scrappable rim

bent to correct and will have to be replaced. If it has an obvious kink, it's probably a scrapper.

Replacing a rim

Even if you don't want to go the whole hog and build a wheel yourself, next time you wreck a rim, you can save yourself some money, and the folks at the bike shop some time, by swapping the rim over for yourself. It also gives you extra wheel building experience, and lets you study how a rim is laced.

Provided the new rim takes the same size spokes (and the folks at the shop will be able to tell you that) you can transfer the spokes across from your old bent rim to your new one. If it's a rear wheel, it's a good idea to remove the freehub sprockets or block before rebuilding it. By the way, it's impossible to remove a freewheel from a hub if it's not built into a wheel, as the wheel is used to turn the hub when using the free-wheel remover. The worst thing you can do is to cut the spokes from the wheel, leaving the freewheel in place.

Tape the new rim to the old one making sure to get the orientation right, with the valve holes in the same place, and the offset spoke holes correctly positioned. Go all the way around your old wheel and loosen all the spokes off so that they're just held in by a couple of turns of the thread in the nipples. Now you can start taking each spoke out of the old rim completely, putting the nipple in the same hole in the new rim and

Replacing a rim

rim, and see the spoke's position inside the thread of the nipple. Correct length spokes come up to the flat in the top of the nipple. Unfortunately older spokes tend to be different lengths due to stretch caused by hard riding. Despite having the same tension, they will cause a wheel to wobble.

If it's a rear wheel, the rim probably hasn't conveniently landed in the centre of the hub. This is because the position of the spokes on

giving it a couple of turns to hold it in place. Once you've got all the spokes in the new holes you can either take it to a bike shop for them to tension it up, or have a go yourself.

Tensioning

For building up a wheel from scratch, a jig and dishing tool are very useful, but I've built more than a couple of wheels in my bike frame alone. The first thing to do is to tighten all the spokes up to the same tension, and this is done easily by checking the amount of thread left at the top of the spoke nipple. Sight down from the

A dished rear wheel. Note that the rim is central in the dropouts, but not in the middle of the spoke flanges

a rear hub isn't the same as on a front one. The rim isn't usually directly between the spoke flanges because the freewheel takes up more room on one side of the hub, resulting in the spokes on that side being more vertical than the spokes on the other side. This asymmetric shape is called 'dish' and what it means to you is that the spoke tension on the freewheel side must by slightly greater than on the non-freewheel side. Add a quarter turn to all the spokes on the freewheel side, and take a quarter turn off the others.

Now it's worth starting to correct vertical and lateral wobbles as we detailed before. Don't worry too much if the wheel still isn't central in the frame as you can correct the sideways movement by tightening the spokes on one side once it's right.

The way to check to see that the wheel is correctly centred in the frame is to measure the distance from a point on the frame to the rim, then turn the wheel round so that it's the wrong way round. Measuring

Using a dishing tool to check for lateral misalignment

from the same frame point to the rim, the distance should be identical. If it's not, don't fret. Just add a quarter turn on one side, take a quarter turn off the other side, and pull the wheel across and try it again.

The only really big stumbling block in all this is the amount of tension the wheel should have in it. It's best to have another well-built wheel to check the tension with. Too much and the wheel can spontaneously fold into a crisp shape, while too little can make the wheel fold when you ride off the first kerb. If you're unsure check with your friendly local wheel builder.

Building from scratch

It's certainly possible to build strong wheels at home, and of all the maintenance aspects of working on your bike, it's probably the most rewarding, but you've got to spend lots of time getting it right. It's not as mystical as it is made out, and if you've got the mechanical aptitude you can learn fairly quickly. Covering it fully would require a whole book in itself. (See Bibliography for further reading).

Starting from scratch with a long way to go – wheelbuilding is a long but rewarding job

Choosing a wheel

When ordering wheels from a shop, it's useful to know what to ask for. Not everybody is suited to 32x16g spokes with a skinny rim. If you're racing, then light wheels are where it's at, and 28-spoke units can stand up well to racing abuse if they're built properly and looked after.

For expedition and rough riding heavier wheels are a good idea. 36 spokes are overkill for a front wheel, but for a rear wheel when the rider spends a lot of time in the air with hard landings, it's a good idea. Top of the heap for super strong rims are the bizarre FIR Impes rim and the new Mavic 131 rim.

Rims did go through a phase of getting incredibly skinny a couple of years ago, and that seems to have calmed down now, with 23mm being accepted as the narrowest it's possible to run real two inch tyres on. If you're running 1.5inch tyres all the time then a 20mm rim is an option, but their performance with two inch tyres leaves a lot to be desired.

Radial spoking is another feature that came and went. Front wheels were laced with spokes coming straight from the hub, rather than tangentially, but with several hub breakages on the circuit, their use has declined. For the record radial lacing does little to increase any wheel performance factors (except looks) and saves around five grams. Wow!

Snowflake lacing with the spokes wrapping round each other has appeared lately, and looks to be a good way of making super-strong light wheels. Time will tell if it catches on. Wheels have been around for a long time, so it's not surprising that real improvements in their performance are few and far between.

10: HEADSETS AND FORKS

Headsets

Mountain bike headsets get hammered. Until recently steering bearing design was one department in which the mountain bike had not evolved significantly from the road bike and, consequently, this often-neglected bearing was one of the parts which needed most frequent attention. An important change in the last year or so has been the introduction of Dia-Compe's Aheadset system, which dispenses with many of the normal components of the headset, reduces weight and makes maintenance easier.

In 1990, mountain bike headsets changed somewhat. The road bike size, which has a one inch diameter steering column, was the standard for almost a decade, but has now been almost completely replaced by two 'oversize' versions, Tioga's 1 1/8inch Avenger size and Fisher's 1 1/4inch Evolution size. These headsets have more and larger bearings than the road bike size and have gone some of the way towards making headsets more durable and reliable.

Whether this was necessary or not is still a bone of contention in some circles, but there's no doubt at all that the Tioga oversize type is now

the *de facto* industry standard for real mountain bikes. The Fisher Evolution size is now rare, probably because parts for it always seemed to be amazingly expensive.

After John wrote about headsets in *Mountain Biking UK* a couple of years ago, he got a letter from a reader asking why no one used taper roller bearings in them, since these have a much greater bearing contact area and would therefore be much more durable. The simple answer was that standard bearings are so much more tolerant of slight errors in the alignment of bearing mounting surfaces that it was much cheaper for manufacturers to use them, than to produce frames and forks that were accurately engineered for a taper-roller headset to work. Since then, Klein's Attitude and Adroit superbikes, which use large aircraft control bearings that cannot be adjusted in the headset, have shown that alternative headset designs can work.

The most recent development in headset design is the aheadset, which went from a bright idea to an industry standard on high end bikes in a matter of months. The aheadset uses a plain steerer tube, rather than a threaded one, and holds the steering bearings in place by clamping the stem round the steerer. It's a clean, elegant design that makes adjusting the headset easier, saves a big chunk of weight and looks good.

Anyway, on with the business at hand. The topic of headsets splits neatly into problem diagnosis, maintenance and lubrication and replacement, so we'll take them in that order.

Problem diagnosis

Aside from the issue of the three different sizes, headsets come in three types stiff (too tight), stiff (bearing damage) and loose. Oh, and working right. *Sutherland's Handbook for Bicycle Mechanics* lists eleven different possible problems and causes for malcontent headsets of which the last is 'Poor quality headset. Some just aren't designed to work.' In our workshop these are known as type eleven headsets and can only be cured by replacement. For other problems, less radical cures exist if the trouble is caught early. If, however, you ride around for two months on a loose headset, don't expect much sympathy from your local shop if it will not run smoothly when you get around to tightening it. Indeed, this goes for all bearings – an ounce of timely prevention can save you pounds of expensive cures.

A loose headset will manifest itself as a shaking or juddering of the forks as you brake, and can be easily checked for by holding the front brake on hard, and rocking the bike

backwards and forwards. If the headset clicks or rocks from one position to another, then it's loose.

A tight headset will not turn smoothly in the head tube, or will exhibit 'click stop' steering. Often the only permanent cure for such units is replacement, but a temporary cure is to replace the caged balls with loose ones, as detailed below.

An over-tight headset can also produce an entertaining mode of steering failure that engineers call 'capsize', which occurs when the bike is unable to turn as much as you need it to when you lean into a turn, with the result that you fall off. Fortunately this tends to be a low-speed problem, but if you feel that your bike isn't handling right in tight, tricky, slow situations, check the headset.

The most serious headset fault is when it is loose or properly adjusted when pointing directly forward, but becomes tight when turned to the side. This is a symptom of a bent steerer tube and indicates that the forks, or at least the steerer, needs replacing.

Tools

The only essential tools are a good pair of thin headset spanners the right size for your headset – Park, Shimano, Campag or the slightly cheaper Leda or Tacx ones. These are not cheap, but do have bottom bracket tools on the other ends, so they kill two birds with one stone.

Old-style one inch road bike

headsets need 32mm spanners, Tioga 1 1/8inch need 36mm jobs, and Fisher Evolution 1 1/4inch headsets require 40mm spanners. The problem of the availability of these tools, which plagued the early days of oversize headsets, has now eased, and any bike shop should be able to get them for you.

Maintenance and lubrication

If your headset is just in need of adjustment, then there's no need to do more than tweak the bearing and tighten the locknut and top race cup against each other.

Hold the top cup in place with one spanner while the locknut is tightened with the other. If a headset will not tighten no matter what you do with it, the fork crown race may be loose; if so it will need replacing. It's also possible that the fork crown race mounting has been cut too small and will need building up with brass and re-cutting. This is a job for a frame builder.

Another reason why a headset will not tighten even though the locknut appears to tighten against something, is that the steering column is too long and the locknut is locking against the top of the steerer rather than the top race. If this is the case it can be diagnosed by dismantling the headset (see below) to remove the locknut, and comparing the height of the locknut to the height of the steerer remaining above the race. If

there is more steerer than locknut, fit a spacer. Catching problems before they become serious is the key to day to day maintenance of headsets. John had a Deore DX headset last three years; regular dismantling, cleaning and bearing replacement kept it smooth as a baby's bum, until one very busy and wet winter did it in.

Dismantling

To do more than merely adjust the headset, for example to lubricate it, it will need dismantling. The first step is to disconnect the front brake then remove the handlebar and stem from the frame, to allow access to the guts of the headset.

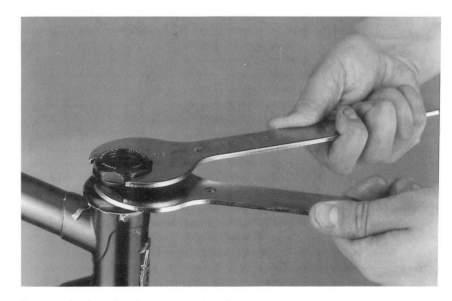

Loosen the headset by unscrewing the locknut anticlockwise, holding the top race with the other spanner. The top cup should then be adjusted by hand so that the forks turn freely and without play — here the stem has been removed for clarity

Loosen the stem by unscrewing the 6mm Allen bolt in the middle of it anticlockwise. Recent designs of stem with a recessed bolt may require you to use the long end of the Allen key in the stem and turn the short end with some sort of lever, like a ring spanner

With the stem out, the headset is dismantled by loosening the locknut and top cup and unscrewing them from the steerer. The fork can then be lowered from the frame

Tap the bolt down with a hammer to release the expander or wedge from the steerer. For standard stems use a piece of wood to protect the top of the bolt from the hammer

This is what you'll find as you take apart your headset. The locknut and top race are separated by a tabbed washer that is essential to keep the adjustment right. The bearings are held in a cage. Remove the caged bearings from the headset and take them to the shop with you when you buy replacements to make sure you get the right size of loose balls. Remove the rubber seals from the top and bottom parts of the headset and put them somewhere safe, noting which goes where and which way up

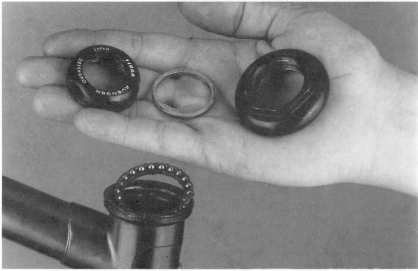

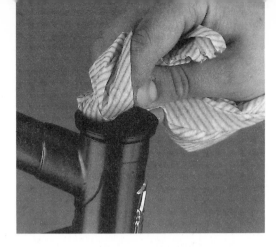

Clean all the bearing surfaces and inspect them for wear or pitting. If any parts are worn you'll probably need to replace the whole headset, since spares are both hard to find and ridiculously expensive

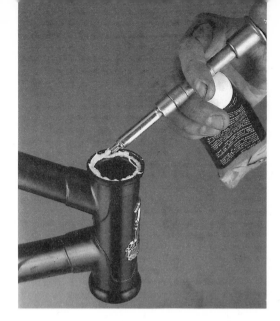

Smear a thick layer of grease into the bottom race cup and place the bearings into it. There should be enough grease to hold them in place. Replace the seal in the cup. Repeat the procedure with the top race cup, since you want it ready to put in place when you insert the forks

Headset assembly

To reassemble the headset you'll need about 55 5/32inch ball bearings for a road-size headset, and enough bearings of the appropriate size for an oversize headset (sorry to be so vague, but the sizes vary between models of headset and it's not unusual to find different sizes top and bottom).

Headsets are one area of a bike where caged bearings are simply not justifiable. Since a headset just takes impact loads, and does not have to turn much, it needs as many bearings as possible to maximise the bearing surface. In addition, oversize headsets use larger bearings than road bike units because the increase in surface area of the bearings increases the total bearing surface faster than the larger diameter reduces it. Most 1 1/8inch oversize headsets use 7/32inch balls, Shimano Deore XT headsets in both one inch

and 1 1/4inch take 1/4inch balls, as do most other 1 1/4inch headsets.

When you buy replacement loose balls, get about twice as many as there are in the cages. Don't worry if they don't all fit; headsets vary and there's an allowance in that number for the inevitable one or two that fall on the floor and disappear!

Insert the forks in the frame, taking care not to dislodge any balls from the bottom race cup, and screw the top race cup down on the forks. Put the tab washer back and screw the locknut down on to the washer. In some headsets the top race cup is threaded on to the steerer rather than installed in the frame, so the balls sit in this cup and care must also be taken to avoid dislodging them

Headset replacement

We have to say that we consider this a job best left to a bike shop. However, if you must know how to do it, here goes. Dismantle the headset as above.

Screw the headset race down on to the cup and adjust the bearing so that it is just not loose. For almost all bicycle bearings the correct adjustment is the most freely turning position at which the bearing is not able to move or rattle. Tighten the locknut against the race, holding the race with the other spanner

Finally, grease the stem, replace it in the steerer and tighten the stem bolt hard

Remove the fork crown race from the fork by lifting it off with a hammer and punch. Tap alternately each of the sides which overlap the fork crown until the race is free of its mounting.

To remove the cups from the frame, tap them out from the inside with a hammer and a piece of half-inch cylindrical steel bar with clean, sharp edges. If there is a burr on the edge which you use to tap the thin cup with, it will slip off, making the job significantly more difficult. Move round the point at which you tap so that the cup comes out evenly

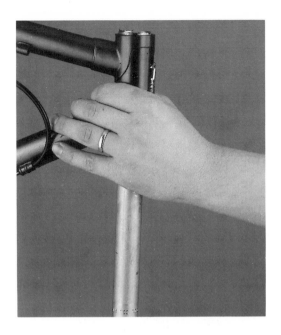

If you are likely to do this job often, which means that you are setting up either a club workshop or a bike shop, Park make a rather useful tool which slips into the head tube and allows you to evenly knock out the headset cups. Its four-flared parts look like fins from a rocket in a 50s sci-fi movie; it is sensibly called a rocket tool and makes the job of fully dismantling a headset much easier.

Take the old headset and the forks with you when you go to buy a replacement. Headsets occasionally differ in the size of the fork crown race mounting and, while most road bike size ones are 26.4mm, a few 27mm ones are still about. 1 1/8inch headsets have 30.0mm fork crown race mounting, while 1 1/4inch units are 33.0mm. The fork crown race is intended to be a tight 'interference' fit on the fork crown. If it drops on easily it is too large.

Stack height

The other potential source of fitting hassle is the issue of 'stack height'. This is the amount of extra steering column length that the headset needs, over and above the length of the head tube. Shimano headsets tend to have very low stack heights and can therefore be replaced only with other Shimano headsets.

One Japanese bike manufacturer, Bridgestone, finds this so annoying that they insert a wide spacer into the Shimano headsets on their bikes so that any headset can be fitted. It is essential to get a headset with the same stack height as the original one, or use spacers to get the locknut to tighten if you are fitting a Shimano headset to a bike that didn't have one.

We don't suggest that you should cut down the steerer to make the new headset fit, because you would then limit your choice of replacement headsets forever. To illustrate the point, road size Shimano headsets typically have stack heights of around 33mm, whereas many headsets are some five or six millimetres higher than this. That few millimetres is difficult to put back once it has been cut off!

To fit the crown race, tap it gently home with the steel bar you used to remove the cups, taking care not to tap the bearing surface, but the flat top edge of the race. A better tool is a piece of tube which fits over the steerer closely so that it cannot slip off. For the photos we used a bit of scrap aluminium from Brant's tool kit, but anything that fits without touching the bearing surface will do. Such a tool also allows you to fit the crown race by the subtle technique of banging the end of the tube on the floor, getting round the problem of how to hold the forks while tapping the race on.

Fitting the cups is best done with a Park, VAR or Campag headset press. They have three-figure price tags and are beyond the means of most. The alternative is to gently tap in the cups with a hammer, placing a wooden block to prevent damage and to spread the load

Reassembly

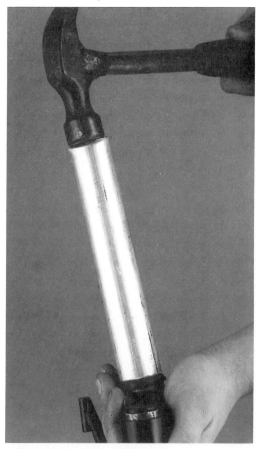

Aheadsets

In many ways Dia-Compe's Aheadset system is the same as a conventional headset: a system of cup and cone surfaces with balls to keep them moving. The bearings are basically the same. The way in which the Aheadset differs from all previous steering bearing systems is in the attachment and adjustment of the bearing. Where a conventional system has a threaded steerer, the Aheadset's is plain. The top race slides on to the steerer and is held in place by the stem, which clamps on to the steerer.

To adjust the bearing, a cap on top of the steerer is pulled down on to the stem by a bolt that screws into a special nut that jams inside the steerer. If all this is as clear as mud, you'll see what we're on about when we rip the parts apart.

The advantages of the Aheadset system are many. Most obviously it saves weight, because the conventional stem's quill and bolt are dispensed with. In theory it is also possible to use a lighter steerer, because a threadless tube is stronger and can therefore be made thinner or from a lighter material. A lightweight Aheadset version of the Rock Shox Mag 21 fork with an aluminium steerer is in development.

The Aheadset system is also easier to adjust when you get used to it. Instead of two heavy spanners you just need a single 5mm Allen key to disassemble and adjust it, at least as far as getting at the bearings goes. Removing the cups and steerer cone requires the same techniques as above. The Aheadset system also abandons the use of threads to align the bearings. Threads aren't the best way to align bearings, since it's difficult to get them perfectly right; the Aheadset's plain steerer system should result in better alignment and therefore longer bearing life.

Changing systems

Many people have asked us if it's worth switching to an Aheadset system. Our answer, on balance, is not straight away. The time to change is when you're changing the fork anyway. At this point a new Aheadset compatible headset and stem will seem like a minor extra expense. To switch to an Aheadset from scratch will cost a new headset and stem, plus a new fork, or at least a new steerer and, possibly, crown. To fit a complete Aheadset system, you need to remove your old headset cups from the frame as detailed above.

Aheadset disassembly

You'll need to dismantle an Aheadset to grease the bearings, change the stem or change the headset parts themselves.

If you peer down inside the steerer you'll see the 'star-fangled nut' that the bolt screws into. When you set up an Aheadset from scratch you hammer this nut into place, 15mm below the top of the steerer. If you botch up and tap it in further than this you'll have to drift it all the way through; it's impossible to back off

Undo and remove the top cap and bolt. These parts are used to adjust the bearing, not to hold the headset together

Top left:
Undo the stem clamp bolt or bolts

Top right:
This Tioga cable hanger clamps into place and therefore needs unbolting. Tioga's Alchemy version of the Aheadset is widely used

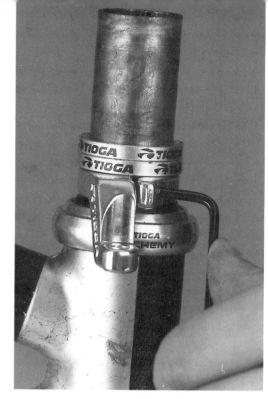

Bottom left:
Lift the stem off the steerer. You can see here the spacers which are typically used to give height adjustment in Aheadset systems, and the cable hanger

Bottom right:
This is what the bits under the spacers look like. The conical piece is a compression ring, under which is the top bearing race and top cup. The compression ring wedges between the steerer and the top race so that the top bearing moves with the steerer. When you take all of this stuff off, the fork falls out of the frame and lands on your foot

Reassembly

This is almost the exact opposite of the disassembly process, but not quite. Put the bearing race, compression ring, spacers and whatnot back on, then slip the stem on. Don't tighten the stem bolt. Put in the top cap and the screw. Very gently tighten the screw. The screw simply pushes the stem and other parts down to load the bearings. Since it has no role in keeping the headset together it only needs to be loaded enough to keep the bearing from rattling. Then tighten the stem bolt(s). We have seen top caps wrecked by over-enthusiastic tightening. It can't be stressed enough that it just needs to be tight enough to hold the bearing together.

If the bearing won't tighten easily, the most likely problem is that the stem is preventing the cap from loading the bearing, or that there is a circlip in the assembly, as used in some Tioga systems. Ditch the circlip − it's not essential − and grease the inside of the stem.

We do not recommend replacing the top cap with an aluminium one. The plastic cap is meant to break if you over-tighten it, to stop you from wrecking a headset by running the bearings too tight. A new plastic cap costs very little, so it's a question of which would you rather write off?

Forks

The fork is the first thing that gets mangled in a front end collision. A properly designed mountain bike should have a fork that fails before the frame, since forks are less expensive than frames, and easier to replace. In recent years some forks have become so over-designed that a frame will fold while the fork cheerfully sits there and takes it; not a sensible design. Unfortunately it is easier to design a super-strong fork than a super-strong frame. A bent fork will manifest itself by causing the headset to become stiff when turned a long way to the side, even though it is smooth within a few degrees of straight ahead. While it is possible to straighten a crash-damaged fork with lots of brute force, this is an emergency, get-you-home measure, and a bent fork should be replaced immediately. A fork that has been bent and then straightened will be severely weakened and could break at any time. It should not be ridden.

To fit a new fork, it first needs to be cut to length. Either measure it against the original fork or assemble it into the frame, fit the top race and allow sufficient threads for the locknut. Mark the point where the fork needs to be cut by making the beginning of a saw cut. Dismantle the fork from the frame and screw a top race on to the thread so that the cutting mark is at the top of the race. Use the race as a guide when cutting the forks down, so that you get a straight cut.

When you've cut off the excess steerer, file the top of it smooth and unscrew the race from the fork. This will push the thread at the top of the steerer back into shape, allowing you to screw a new one on. Clean any metal filings off the fork and — especially — the crown race before reassembling the headset.

If there is insufficient thread on the steerer to enable you to trim it to length without running out of thread, you will need to get extra thread cut on the fork. This really is a job for an experienced bike shop mechanic. Cutting fork threads involves using a special tool, and takes about 20 minutes per inch if you know what you're doing. If you don't know what you're doing you will produce a ragged thread that won't take a headset and will ruin the fork. Far safer to put the job into sure hands and pay for the reassurance that it's their problem if anything goes wrong.

Fork choice

There was a lot of fuss about rigid fork designs a couple of years ago, so Brant did some testing of the different aftermarket forks which produced some interesting results.

For a start, it doesn't seem to matter whether a fork is straight or curved. A fork is a cantilevered beam, and how it gets from the crown to the hub seems to make no difference to the way the fork absorbs shock. Since most mountain bike forks are pretty rigid in a straight line, and tyres are not, most of the shock absorption in a standard front end seems to go on in the tyre.

What matters more is the fork's resistance to torsional deflection, and this is determined by the size and configuration of the fork blades themselves. In short, wide diameter fork blades resist twisting better than thin ones and therefore give better handling, a point to bear in mind when choosing new forks.

The big issue at the moment, though, is suspension. There are dozens of suspension forks available, and we deal with the maintenance requirements of the three most common in the next chapter.

11: SUSPENSION FORKS

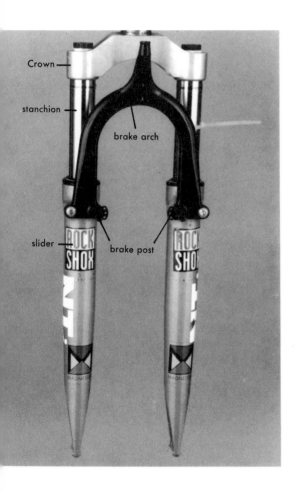

Crown
stanchion
brake arch
slider
brake post

A pair of Rock Shox

The advent of suspension forks has brought a whole new area of maintenance, requiring a new level of skill from riders and mechanics. Suspension forks aren't all that tricky to maintain, they just need different methods from those practised on any other part of your bike.

There is also some new terminology for suspension forks. The machined aluminium clamp holding everything in place is called the triple clamp. Clamped into the triple clamp are chrome plated stanchion tubes, and sliding on the stanchions are the sliders.

If you are going to delve deep into the innards of your forks, you need to know a little about what goes on inside. Suspension forks can be split into two categories when it comes to describing their internal workings. Air/oil forks use a combination of an air spring and oil damping to control their movement. The oil can get polluted by dirt being sucked into the fork by the action of damping and springing which provides the shock absorption. When the oil gets dirty the forks stop working efficiently, and the internals can deteriorate badly.

Elastomer forks use small rubber cylinders to provide the suspension medium. These rubbers do degrade with time, but it's usually more a problem that the bearing surfaces have become dirty. Elastomer forks are made by, amongst others Manitou, Pace, Pro-Forx, Rock Shox Quadra and Tange. Air/oil forks include Rock Shox Mag and RS range, and Marzocchi.

Lifting the dust seals lets you check underneath for bits of dirt. Blow these out and it will save you the job of stripping the forks down frequently

Check that the bolts are securely holding the brace to the sliders. These bolts are held in place with loctite, so if they're not loose in the threads, they're OK

Regular Maintenance

You can reduce the frequency of fork maintenance by keeping your forks clean. Certain forks can be fitted with shock-boots, to keep the muck out of the bearings. Indeed, several forks don't have lip-seals on the sliders, but instead rely on boots to keep the muck out. This has the advantage of reducing fork stiction in operation, but the boots must seat properly to keep the dirt out. If you're retrofitting boots to your suspension forks, don't be tempted to firmly zip tie shock boots in place. Their closed bellows act like a suction pump, and have been known to suck the lubricant out of the forks.

Pace RC-35 forks aren't designed to work with boots, as they have excellent seals and their travel uses up all the space on the stanchion. With Rock Shox Mag 20/30 there isn't a lot of room at the back of the fork brace to accommodate the shock boots. Either space them off the sliders with a 1-2mm thick washer, or cut a hole in the boots. Mag 21s have enough room for boots, and indeed boots are an optional extra that we recommend you use.

Regular maintenance on Rock Shox is a matter of lifting the dust seal at the top of the fork, and getting rid of the nasties from underneath. Dirt sitting in here can wander down into the fork leg, contaminating the oil in the fork which performs the damping function.

Every week or so, check the

tightness of all the bolts on your forks to ensure nothing has come loose. The bolts are held securely into the fork with Loctite, so there's no need to tighten the bolts further, just check that the Loctite hasn't broken down and caused a component to start wobbling

Full Servicing

Every now and then, forks need a complete strip down to their barest parts to ensure that they work properly. As with any product, it's hard to spot the gradual degradation of performance, but if your mates have got similar components of different ages, you can check your forks by bouncing up and down on them. Do yours feel strange. Gritty and clicky? Do they leak? Do they make strange gurgling noises? Do they fail to move at all? If they do, you need to have a good look inside and find out what's wrong.

Servicing Pace RC-35 fork

Pace's elastomer forks are now in their second incarnation, and there are a couple of differences in the internal design. However both models are essentially the same to get into. First, disconnect the brakes, by quick releasing the cantilever, and undoing the brake cable from the rocker and cantilever. With the bike upside down, pull the plastic caps from the bottom of the sliders. This gives access to the retaining bolts.

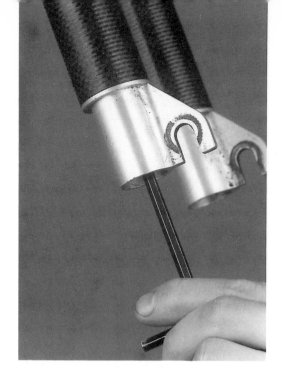

Pace forks are dismantled with an Allen key. Undoing this screw lets you pull off the sliders, revealing the elastomer suspension cores and the stanchions

Undo the bolt in each leg with an Allen key.

The 1993 and new 1994 Atmosphere Balanced forks need a 4mm Allen Key, RC-35s need a 5mm. Pull the sliders upwards to remove them from the stanchions. RC-35s have elastomer core rods, to hold the elastomers in place, whereas AB forks have a custom screw and internal valve retaining the elastomers. Clean the forks in warm soapy water. I use washing up liquid, and rinse the forks thoroughly afterwards. It's OK to put the forks back together with a little water in it, but all traces of degreaser should be removed or it will break down the lubricant in the fork.

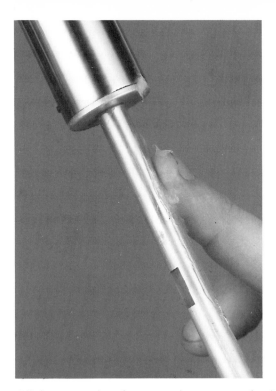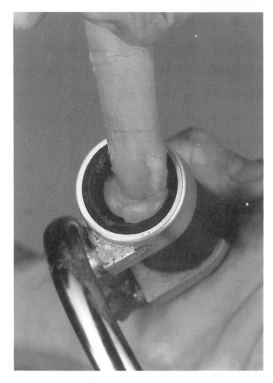

All the internal surfaces need coating with silicone grease or the new Pace grease to stop damage from abrasion

On RC-35s the core rods, the top-out chamber and the bearing surfaces on the sliders all need coating. Similarly, the guide rod on AB forks needs lubricating in the same manner, along with the inside of the top-out chamber. Re-installation is simple.

On RC-35s, replace the elastomers on the guide rods, ensuring they are the same on both sides. Refit the sliders, over the stanchions, taking care not to chew the seals up on fitting. The top-out rubber must be replaced, followed by the washer and Allen bolt. Do not tighten this bolt down hard. It only needs to be nipped tight, and this is best achieved whilst exerting a little down force on the

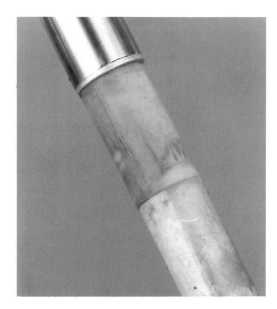

Before you slide the sliders back onto the stanchions, slide the elastomers onto the core rods. With RC35 AB forks, the elastomers need to be pushed into the sliders, and the long screw fitted up the inside

fork brace to compress the elastomers.

RC-35 ABs are slightly different. Push the elastomers into the sliders, with the cross-flow valve between them, then place the sliders onto the stanchions. Slide them downwards, again ensuring that you don't chew up the seals. The screw fits right through the elastomers into the stanchions, and the top out rubber is fitted with an acetol washer above it. Again do not over tighten, and again, push down on the brace to compress the elastomers, before nipping the bolt tight. Replace the caps, reconnect the brakes, and you're ready to ride.

Servicing Rock Shox

Unlike the simplicity of elastomer technology, Rock Shox use full-on suspension techniques of air springs and oil damping. Because of this the maintenance requirements are different from those found on any other area of the bike. It's not hard, just different!

The task is complicated by the fact that there have been five different versions of the Rock Shox fork to date. The original Rock Shox was introduced in 1990 and is now known as the RS-1. In 1992 Rock Shox produced the Mag 20, which had a dial to adjust the damping, and the Mag 30, which didn't. Problems with frequent servicing and reliability led to the 1993 Mag 21, a considerably better fork which for our money, is the best one currently available. The current version without a damping

dial is called the Mag 10 which is similar to the Mag 30. Rock Shox without damping dials have a plastic cover over the air hole in the top of the fork.

The only maintenance job that is suitable for the home mechanic is changing the oil. Delving further into the forks is considerably harder and requires special Rock Shox tools. Call the importer and ask for details. The oil should be changed when it starts degrading and becoming a cacky colour. For weekend riders, this is probably once a year, but if you ride and train frequently, it could be as often as once every two months. Shockboots notably prolong the time between services, but frequent oil changes will prolong the life of the internals.

To change the oil remove the wheel, brakes and brake arch from the fork legs. The bolts holding the fork brace in place are usually secured with Loctite, so it may take a fair amount of force to break the bond Remove the brake posts as well. Clean the exterior of the fork legs, to stop any internal contamination

Remove the screws in the valve at the top of the fork leg, loosen the bolts in the fork crown and now remove the fork legs from the crown.

Now you must depressurise the fork. Unscrew the needle from your Rock Shox pump and insert it into the fork. Allow the air to drain off, pointing the needle away from your face to avoid the oil mist. Mag 10, Mag 30 and RS 1s have a pop-in cap at the top of the fork that will need to be removed before this can be done.

Remove the Rock Shox brake posts and the bolts holding the brace to the slider. This lets you access each leg individually, and makes maintenance and removal much easier

Remove the screw that seals the aircap, and insert a football needle into the valve. This lets you depressurise the fork. Failing to do this would mean getting sprayed with oil at the next step

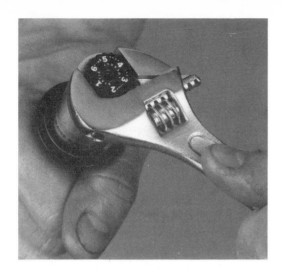

This gives you access to the oil, and you should be able to check the colour. It starts off red, so if it's a dark red, it's on its way out, and if it's black, then you are in trouble, and the whole fork should be stripped and cleaned. This is a shop job.

Provided the fork legs are OK, it's time to drain off the oil. Pour it into a bottle, and pump the legs to get all the oil out. You can even leave them upside down for a while to get it all out. Please dispose of the old oil carefully in an environmentally friendly way.

Now compress the stanchion completely into the slider. In Mag 20 and 21s turn the adjuster rod to the full anti-clockwise position using the air cap, and add the replacement oil.

Use only fork shock specific oil, that is Automatic Transmission Fluid (ATF, SAE 8wt). Fill the oil to within an inch of the top of the tube. Pump the stanchion up and down until no air pockets are felt, usually about ten times. Now with the stanchion fully compressed into the slider, add or remove oil until the fluid level is correct: Mag 21/10 40mm; Mag 20/30 35mm; RS-1 45mm

Next remove the air cap. Mag 20s and 21s need a 19mm spanner, or better still, a 19mm socket. For the others, push the cap down into the leg 10mm, remove the wire clip, screw a long 6mm bolt into the air cap hole and use it to pull the cap up. Ensure the walls of the tube aren't scratched whilst this is being done, as this will ruin the air seal

Pour away the contaminated oil into a jar, and dispose of it carefully. This is the best way to gauge the wear of your forks. If the oil is red then it's OK. If it's gunky and brown or black, then there has been a lot of dirt in there, and other internal problems could have occurred

Refill the fork with the correct weight, and the correct type of oil. Special suspension fork oil must be used, not vegetable oil, not chain oil, not Olive Oil

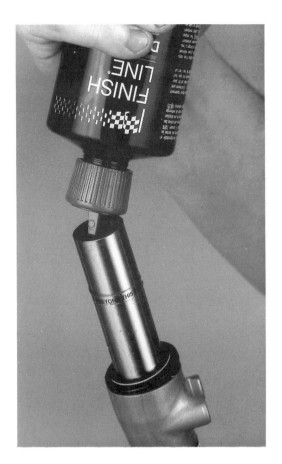

Servicing Manitou forks

Doug Bradbury's Manitou fork is the other popular elastomer fork. Getting at the insides is a bit more complicated than for the Pace fork because you have to use a long Allen key to undo the bolt that holds the fork together, getting at it from the top of the stanchion, rather than the bottom of the slider.

Release the brakes and remove the straddle cable from the hanger. There is no need to remove the fork

This fluid level is measured from the top of the fluid to the top of the stanchion. We did this by poking a clean screwdriver into the stanchion, and seeing where the oil came up to. Ensure that it is the same at both sides.

Now replace the air cap, by screwing it in place, in the case of the Mag 20 or 21. With the others, slide the air cap into the fork, 5mm past the wire clip groove. Lube the O ring seal with grease, install the wire clip and compress the stanchion to seat the air cap. Pressurise the forks to 80-100psi and leave for one hour, after which the pressure can be lowered to the required setting

other fork leg, the forks can be pulled apart. Slide the forks down the stanchions, and pull them off the end. They may need a firm tug to remove them. Now you'll have the forks in two parts

Clean and dry the sliders thoroughly, and apply a coat of light grease to the bearing surfaces. If you remove the elastomers from the guide rod, check that there is a compression washer between each one.

Reassembly of the forks is the tricky bit. Don't slide the lower long

Refitting all the bolts and brake posts correctly is easy. Make sure that the brake posts go on the inside hole, and also use a spot of Loctite Threadlock to stop the fixings rattling loose on the brace. When clamping the stanchions back into the crown, ensure that the tubes are level, and that they don't go below the recommended level in the crown

bridge for the removal of the sliders. Getting inside these forks requires an 11inch long 5mm Allen Key.

Pop the caps off the top of the stanchions with a screwdriver, insert the Allen key into the socket in the bottom of the stanchion, and unscrew it.

If you have Manitou 2 forks, you'll need to hold the pre-load adjuster on the bottom of the forks to stop it turning. After repeating this on the

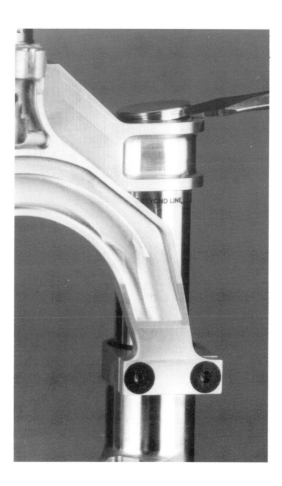

Prise off the Manitou top caps to allow entry to the Allen bolt holding the elastomers in place

Using the long 11inch Allen key provided, unscrew the rod holding the elastomers in place. Manitou 2 users may have to hold the adjusters at the bottom of the fork to stop them spinning

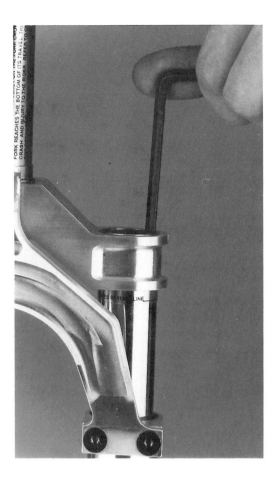

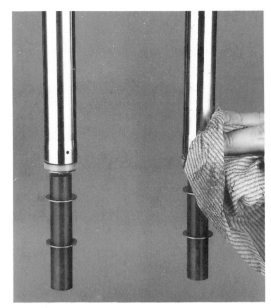

Wipe the stanchions clean before greasing them with a coat of light grease. See how the elastomers are arranged with washers between each one

elastomer any more than half way onto the guide rod. Also, ensure that the bushing that mounts on the end of the stanchion isn't fitted on its stop. Slide the elastomers into the fork, past the upper bushing, and then slide the lower bushing past the upper bushing, ensuring that it locates on the sides of the slider. Push down on the forks and you should feel and hear a 'clunk' as the lower bushing locates onto the end of the stanchion. Now you need to tighten the guide bolts to the end stop, not too tight. The short Allen key extension provides enough torque.

Push the lower bushing off its stop, and drop it into the fork leg. When the forks are slid together, they will clunk in place as the bushing aligns on this stop

Setting up

Suspension forks come set up for the average rider, in average terrain. As the average rider doesn't exist you can bet that your forks aren't right for you. All you need to help you get the best performance from your forks is a zip tie fastened around one of the stanchions.

By sliding the zip tie down until it is resting on the fork seal, when you've been for a ride the maximum travel will be shown by the zip tie. Go for a ride and try it. Ride just as you normally do, and then measure the distance from the seal to the bottom of the zip tie. Compare this to the maximum travel that is attainable on your fork. Is it less than 70% of the maximum? If so, your forks are too hard. When full travel occurs on some forks you can feel a hard bottom out, but some elastomer suspension forks never reach a fixed bottom out, the elastomers just decide that they don't want to compress any more. Anyhow, if the measurement from seal to zip tie is more than 90% of the maximum, it may be worth your while increasing the hardness of the forks.

Elastomer forks change their stiffness by swapping elastomers. The pre-load that can be set on some forks doesn't adjust the stiffness of the movement, just the point at which the forks start moving. Air/oil forks let you change stiffness by altering the pressure inside the main chamber. Whatever forks you have, ensure that you do the same to both sides!

Air/oil forks can also use different weights of oil to alter the damping characteristics of the fork. This is getting too complicated for a general maintenance book, but information is available from the importers.

We haven't covered rear suspension here. For a number of reasons. First there are so many different systems available that a really comprehensive look at them would almost require a small book in itself. Second, the current crop of rear suspension bikes are, at best, one and a halfth generation designs. There's a maxim in computer software that says: Only a fool buys anything less than version three. And the only bike that has reached version three as yet is the Offroad Proflex. We expect to see some really sorted suspension designs for 1994.

12: PEDALS

If there's a part on a mountain bike which should cause frequent problems, it's the pedals. No other moving part of the bike gets as near to the ground, or immersed in streams, puddles and liquid mud as frequently as the pedal bearings, and pedals are often the first part of the bike to land when you take a tumble.

As mountain bikes have developed, so have pedals, and they're currently far technically advanced from the simple platform and toestrap that were the vogue when mountain bikes began riding in the dirt. Clipless pedals, which lock the foot like a ski-binding are where it's at for serious off road riding, giving more freedom and comfort than any high-end conventional pedal. That said, there's still room for conventional pedals on the market. Clipless models aren't cheap, and the vast majority of bikes come with conventional pedals and straps.

Conventional pedals rule the roost for first time riders, riders with a limited budget and riders who don't look after their bikes too well. With a complicated latch mechanism, clipless pedals don't work too well with lots of mud and maltreatment. Don't feel you can't ride with conventional pedals, it's just that we like Shimano Pedalling Dynamics (SPDs) a lot more. Unlike clipless pedals for roadies, the cleat is recessed into the sole of the shoe and makes walking about much easier.

Similar problems

There are a bunch of problems that afflict both conventional and clipless pedals, not least of which is the horror of the seized pedal. Badly adjusted bearings will show in the same way with either play in the bearings, or a graunchy, gritty feel as you rotate the body. Check for play by grabbing the crank arm and rocking the pedal body. This isolates any play which may be occurring in the bottom bracket. If there's a sign of looseness, check the pedals out, as it certainly isn't going to get any better with time.

If you're hearing clicking noises when you pedal, it's worth checking that your pedals aren't the problem before you dive into your bottom bracket and get really messy. I once had an incessant click on my bike, and subsequently found out it was my knees that were the problem!

To remove a pedal from the crank you require a thin 15mm spanner. Most sets of bottom bracket tools have a 15mm pedal spanner at one end, but a good standard spanner will do just as well.

Adjustable spanners don't usually fit in the narrow gap between pedal cage and crank arm. Some higher quality pedals also have provision for installation with a 6mm Allen key. These are usually fine for installing pedals, but due to the next little problem, removal is a little more tricky.

Due to the pedalling forces on them, the right-hand pedal has a right-hand thread and so unscrews (conventionally) anticlockwise, and the left-hand pedal has a left-hand thread, so unscrews in a clockwise direction. All this gets a bit confusing so just remember that when removing pedals, the top of the spanner or Allen key wants to rotate to the back of the bike. Pedals are always harder to remove than to install, as the forces from pedalling wind them into the crank arms. So it's important, to have a layer of grease on the threads to avoid seizing, and it's not necessary to really wind down hard on the spanner when replacing them on the bike.

If the pedals are stuck, give the end of the axle a good dousing with WD-40 or a similar thin penetrating oil. A sharp tap from a hammer on the spanner may help things on their way, but if it still doesn't come, it's best to leave it to an expert. That said, if you're feeling confident, you might feel like trying a little harder.

If you remove the crank from the bike, you can grip the crank arm in a vice and exert a little more welly on the spanner. It's best to use soft-jaws or bits of wood to avoid scarring the crank whilst doing this. If this doesn't work, the final tip is to heat

the crank arm. This can be done pretty well with a hair dryer, rather than having to use a flame which could concentrate heat dangerously on the pedals.

If you do wreck a crank whilst doing this, don't fret too much. Put it down to experience, remember to grease the threads next time, and buy a single crank from your dealer. By the same token, if your dealer wrecks your crank trying to remove it for you, it isn't his fault, as you shouldn't have been such a bad mechanic in the first place.

Pedals seize because corrosion causes the aluminium of the crank to expand and trap the axle, since rust is weaker than steel, a badly corroded loose pedal could strip the thread out of the crank as it comes. Some dealers may be able to install pedal thread bushes to replace the thread. Others may not. Call around if your cranks are particularly pricey.

A special pedal spanner helps when removing the pedals, and removing the pedals certainly helps when maintaining them. Some can be taken off with a 6mm Allen key from the back of the crank

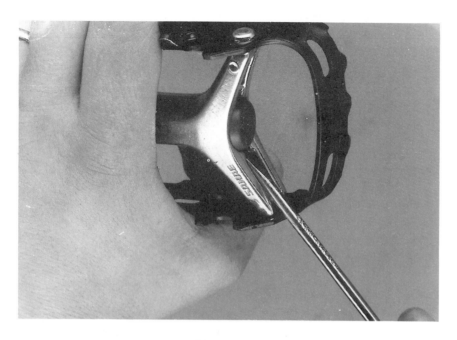

Dustcaps should be easy to take off, but invariably they're not. Use a screwdriver and a dose of common sense and they should come out eventually

Dismantling

Having got the dustcap off, you now need to dismantle the bearings themselves. Inside the pedal you can see the heads of two nuts. These are commonly 10mm and 12mm, although other sizes are not unknown and you'll basically need a set of small metric socket spanners to be sure of getting exactly the right size.

To remove the outer nut (locknut) hold the axle with a spanner or an Allen key, and unscrew it anticlockwise. Do not lose this nut! It's a smaller size than most nuts of the same thread and really rather rare.

There may be a tab washer under this nut, which needs wiggling with a screwdriver to get it off. The cone underneath is the easiest bit to remove, but it requires a slightly unorthodox technique. Some can be removed with a socket spanner, but we've found the best way is to spin it off the axle with a flat-blade screwdriver, while you turn the axle at the other end.

When the cone is out the axle can be removed, allowing the bearings to run all over the floor. Clean everything with solvent, and replace anything that is worn. Cheap pedals aren't worth having to find replacement axles for if they are worn, but ball bearings are an easy fix to get better performance. Typically they're 1/8inch in size, and there are 25 per pedal. Deore and Deore XT are 3/32inch — pretty damn tiny. Take some along to the shop and get the Saturday boy to

Conventional dustcaps

Having removed the pedal from the bike, it's time to do the apparently simple operation of removing the dustcaps . . . except it's not.

There's no real technique for removing dustcaps. Lever, twist or screw the caps until they pop out. Usually there is a gap in the cap for screwdriver insertion. Sometimes there is a serrated cap to twist. Sometimes they are black, shiny and firm. Do your best. Don't do too much damage as dustcaps for anything other than Shimano and Suntour pedals are incredibly hard to replace. Try looking in the shop's scrap bits bin.

Also at this stage, it's worth removing the pedal cage from the body; only possible if it's held in place with Allen key fixings. If it is, remove it.

measure them for funnies.

Pedal bearings are the most likely parts to get hit by water, so the best way to protect them is to fill them with grease. After all, if they're full of grease, the water can't get in! Really thick grease is best, marine quality is excellent, but it's now available for bikes under the Black Gold name. Smear some grease on the races and then pop the bearings in place. Stick the axle through, and then gob loads of grease on top. Fit the cones, the locknut and now you're ready to adjust them.

Adjustment

This is where it all gets really nasty. Unlike all the other bearings on the planet, it's not possible to hold the cone whilst tightening down the

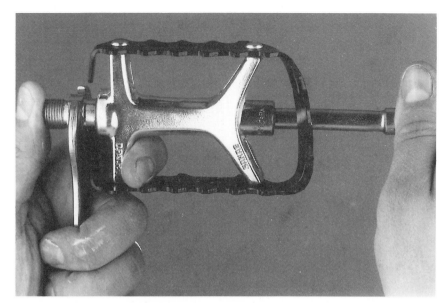

Holding the pedal axle with a spanner, unlock the locknut and keep it somewhere safe. The locknut holds the cone in place, ensuring that the bearings don't loosen

We don't use tons of grease for clarity, but you can pack as much of the stuff into the pedals as possible. Heavy grease is the best

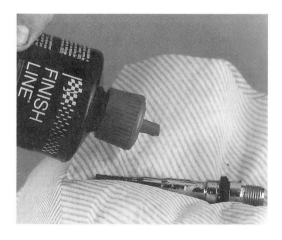

Degreaser helps to cut through the goo, and lets you check the wear on the components. It's worth replacing the ball bearings, as worn balls lead to worn components

locknut on a pedal, resulting in a cat-and-mouse chase for bearing perfection. You get the pedals running nicely, and then tighten the locknut down half a turn to get them secure and they click round like a football rattle. Pedal adjustment can only be done by trial and error, and basically it involves setting the cone slightly loose, and then using the locknut to tighten the cone, holding it in place.

The locknut must be secure to stop the pedal loosening on the first ride. Use the flat-blade screwdriver to turn the cone, and tighten it down with the spanner. Patience is the key here, as it may take four or five attempts to get the tension right. Push or screw the dustcap back in place, and replace the pedal body if you removed it. Grease the pedal threads and screw them back into the crank (checking that it's the right pedal).

Clipless pedals

Introduced towards the end of 1990, clipless pedals have improved the performance of mountain bikes noticeably. Using a miniaturised ski-binding system, the pedals clip onto a 'cleat', a metal plate which is bolted to the underside of a specially produced pair of shoes. The cleat allows the rider to pull up hard on the pedals without the fear of accidental release, yet in an emergency they can release simply by rotating their foot and causing the pedal to release the cleat.

This means that the rider is in far better control of the bike, and crashes caused from coming unattached from the bike have lessened considerably. Sometimes clipless pedals do let you down by not releasing when you want them to, but I won't ride with anything else.

The market is currently dominated by the Shimano SPD system, outweighing other clipless pedals by an incredible factor. For this reason, only maintenance of SPD pedals is covered.

Affectionately known by some as SPuDs, I've been riding with a set for over two years, and have only taken the bearings apart twice to adjust and maintain them, and have dismantled the clip mechanism once out of curiosity.

Maintaining the bearings

SPD's have extremely well-sealed bearings, which are reasonably simple to service when the need arises. The guts are hidden inside the body, with the axle being part of a cartridge unit containing the bearings, which screws directly into the pedal body.

Just as with conventional units, remove the pedals from the bike,

Using the plastic tool you should have got with your SPD's, remove the bearing cartridge. Some early models were prone to snapping the collar, but most are OK. Check the direction of rotation from the marks on the collar

126

with a 15mm spanner, pushing the top of the spanner towards the back of the bike. Now holding the pedal body in your hand, and using the plastic tool provided, turn the tool with a spanner in the opposite direction to the 'tighten' arrow. This pulls the axle and bearing unit from the body on a fine thread, revealing a bearing cartridge, which can be serviced more easily than a regular pedal.

It is possible to dismantle further, but there really is no need, as the bearings are so well protected, all that you need to do is change the grease. Adjusting the bearings can be done with the cone and locknut at the end of the axle, with XT SPDs taking a 7mm and 10mm spanner, and DX SPDs taking an 8mm and 11mm spanner. Adjustments are best achieved whilst the pedal axle is held on a 6mm Allen key clamped in a vice. Free play can be checked by rocking the long silver-coloured spacer.

Now the clever bit. There's no need to dismantle everything to regrease the pedals as they can do it themselves with a little help. Because the axle fits into a cylinder, after cleaning the inside of the pedal body, you can put clean grease into the pedal body, so that when you screw the axle cartridge back into place, the clean grease forces out the old dirty grease, and helps protect the bearings. Wipe off the excess, putting a spot of the mucky grease onto the pedal threads before fitting back onto the bike.

If you desperately want to

Replacing the top plates on SPD's is the only major maintenance they need. With a change of plates every year, the pedals run for ages

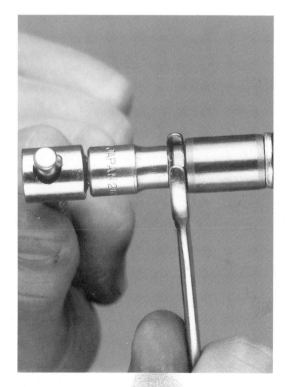

It's a little cramped in the bearing department of an SPD, so thinner spanners than normal may be needed. Play in the bearing can be checked by rocking the silver-steel bearing spacer

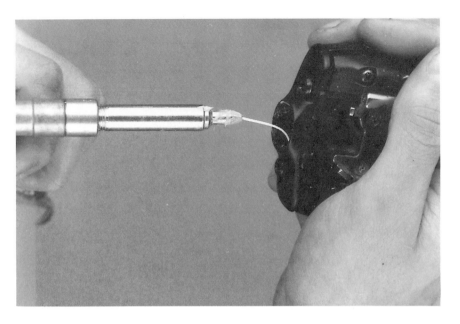

This is a great way to grease your bearings: squirt lots of grease into the hole in the pedal body, then screw in the axle cartridge

dismantle the innards further, then OK. Removing the locknut and cone with the appropriate spanner, the top set of bearings can be removed, then the tubular bearing bit can be pulled off to reveal a plastic spacer holding everything in line. The bottom cone is under the tubular bit, with more bearings.

Replacing cleats

SPD cleats do wear. In around six months of regular use, a cleat wears to the point that it becomes tricky to dismount because the cleat is no longer forcing the pedal catch open enough to let you get out. For good

clicking, keep the cleat area of your shoe free from muck and your pedals clean, and replace your cleats when it all gets a bit tricky.

Replacing top plates

The top plates of SPDs wear with time, and this shows up if you have difficulty removing a new cleat from your pedal. They're held in place with two screws front and back, and have a very thin shim plate underneath. Take care when removing these screws, as it's easy to chew them up and then you'd have to resort to drilling and heli-coiling inserts and many other nasty things.

Knee problems

Clipless pedals do keep your feet more solidly planted than other pedal systems, which is great for most people, but some riders do find that the limited movement possible with clipless pedals causes havoc with their knees.

Ensure that the cleat on the shoe is correctly adjusted for you, which means that knee pains shouldn't happen. If you just can't get it right, maybe you should switch to another system so your knees can recover.

13: BARS AND STEMS

Bars and stems have come a long way since the early days of mountain biking when one-piece units called 'Bullmoose' bars were the order of the day. They were a stem and handlebar in one unadjustable heavy unit. They were however, very strong. Manufacturers briefly used cast or forged aluminium stems, but the most common stem construction technique is the 'pipe stem', made from welded aluminium, steel or titanium.

Bars too have developed, with better production techniques and superior alloys reducing the weight of the average handlebar from 500g to 150g in a few years. Bars are available in different materials too, but for the most part nowadays are aluminium. Bar ends are a now accepted part of mountain bike componentry since their inception in 1990. These clamp on handlebar extensions let you get a more powerful grip for hill climbing or cruising.

Handlebars

Selecting

There are several reasons why you may want to change your handlebars. You may have bent them in a crash, you may be uncomfortable about their position, or you may wish to change them for a lighter model. I suppose you might even dislike the colour . . . who knows!

Bars are available in a variety of materials, lengths and angles. The angles bent into bars should match that of your wrists. Three degrees is comfortable for most, but some casual rider may prefer anything up to 12 degrees. Try them and see.

Many production bikes have very heavy bars, and switching to a light bar could save 4–5oz in some cases. But a word of caution. Since Answer Products introduced the Taperlite bar in 1990 which caused a ripple through the handlebar world, people have been hacking grams off their handlebar weights to win customers. But all this has started to go wrong, with bars snapping during rides, resulting in horrific injuries.

Removing the handlebar grips is one of the most deceptively tricky problems known. Squirt water under them and generally haul them about until they pop off. Hairspray is good for making them stick on again afterwards

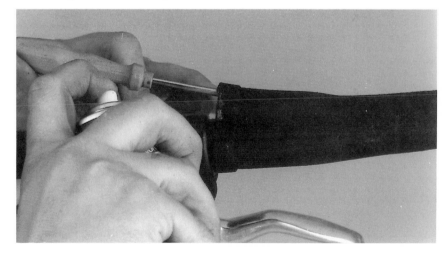

There are a whole bunch of bars available that aren't strong enough for mountain bike use, but they're being sold as such. Most light bars are fine for a couple of months, but as the alloy fatigues, the bars weaken and snap. All aluminium weakens in this way, it's just that handlebars that don't have a lot of aluminium can't be strong for long. Be wary of any handlebar which weighs less than 140g, unless it comes from a very reputable manufacturer and is made in the UK or US. Far Eastern bars weighing under 140g are well dodgy.

Fitting

To fit new bars you fairly obviously have to remove the old ones. The biggest problem isn't getting the brakes or the shifters off, it's removing the grips! I usually stick a thin-bladed screwdriver between the grip and the bar and then squirt in water from a waterbottle. After much squidging and tugging around they usually come flying off.

The other alternative is to simply cut the grips off and replace them. Loosen the brake and gear lever bar clamps and slide them off the ends of the bars. If the cables are so short that you can't do this, loosen the handlebar in the clamp on the stem so that you can slide the bars across to create some slack.

Slide the controls back into the correct positions and angle them at them down at 30–40deg. Fitting the grips and getting them to stay there is tricky; foam grips used to come

with their own glue, but the newer, better rubber models don't. A variety of materials can be used including hairspray, degreaser, oil, petrol, or spray paint. Hairspray is the safest and easiest to use, just squirt large amounts into the end of the grip and push it onto the bar. Before you ride the bike ensure that the grips are dry, and the brakes are connected back properly.

Trimming the bars

Small riders, especially small women, aren't comfortable spreadeagled in the crucifix position that the bars on many production bikes tend to dictate. Don't imagine for a minute that you have to keep your bars the same as when you bought the bike. They can be cut down to a personal fit, but first a few guidelines for customising your position:

- **Wide bars have regained favour with riders this year; don't ask why it just happened. 23inch is the normal width for a male of average height.**
- **Women tend to require narrower bars, but we'd recommend going no narrower than 21inches.**
- **Bar ends take up space on the bars; remember this when fitting them.**
- **The combination of narrow bars and a long stem makes the bike feel very strange at low speed.**

Some stems like this Velocity model have a double bolt clamp to ensure that the bars are held securely. They are a little more tricky to fit the bars through, but nothing too hard.

To fit the new bars, simply reverse the procedure. A useful tip for fitting new bars without scratching them is to spring the stem apart to let them fit through more easily. This can either be done by poking a large flat-blade screwdriver in the gap in the stem clamp and levering gently.

Stems

Selecting

If you're unhappy with the shape, weight, colour or taste of your current stem, then replace it. As with handlebars there's a dizzying array of possibilities on the market, from steel welded models from Tioga, aluminium models from Answer, to shock absorbing pivoting off-road Flexstems.

Riders with oversize headsets obviously need to look for corresponding oversize stems to fit in the fork, though shims are available

to fit small stems in a large fork. Currently there are many different stems on the market, so this shouldn't be a problem. Aheadset users can also have fun trying to find the right after market stem for their bike.

A stem consists of a steerer tube which fits inside the fork, with a V wedge which locks the stem in place when tightened down by a bolt. The extension tube is welded to the steerer, and holds the bar clamp at the correct reach and rise. Stems are measured in terms of reach and rise: reach is the horizontal distance from the centre of the steerer to the bar clamp; rise is the angle of the extension to the steerer tube. Aheadset stems simply clamp onto the steerer tube.

Stems differ not only in size, but also in their method of routing the front brake cable. Some models have internal rollers, while some have external rollers, a fixed stop, or no mounting at all. Internal rollers fell out of fashion because they caused the cable to fray unless installed perfectly. Good stems come from Salsa, Answer, Syncros and Orange.

Here, we are just like we said, prising the stem clamp apart to get the bars in without scratching them. It's not just vanity either; lightweight bars can snap because of deep scratches in their surface

Fitting

If you want to replace your stem, you'll have to remove your bars first, though if you're cunning you should only have to disturb one side of the bars to slide the stem off.

A stem is held in place by the action of the wedge tightening against the chamfer on the steerer tube. To loosen the stem you need to 'unlock' these two components. Slacken the Allen bolt in the quill a couple of turns, then tap the bolt with a hammer, protecting it with a piece of wood. This should knock the wedge down in the steerer tube, releasing the stem and allowing you to remove it from the fork.

After releasing the front brake, grip the front wheel between your knees, and twist the handlebars from side to side while pulling upwards. The stem should pull out of the forks easily. If it doesn't then you'll need to squirt some WD-40 or similar down the gap between the stem and the steerer tube and leave it to soak for a while. If it still doesn't budge, it's down to the shop for the judicious application of some brute force.

The first line of attack is to turn the bike upside down in a workshop stand, fill the inside of the steerer with penetrating oil and leave it to marinade overnight. Then, clamp the fork crown in a vice and attempt to turn the bars, perhaps with a long tube over the end of the bar for extra leverage. If this doesn't work, you usually have to take the decision to write off the stem, saw off the top of it and use heat or chemical means to remove the lump of stem which remains. Alloy stems can be dissolved out with caustic soda, steel stems heated till they submit. A thoroughly seized stem is likely to be unusable by the time it's out; the forks usually survive, though we have seen road bike forks bend under the force needed to free a really recalcitrant stem. Such problems for Aheadset users; just release the clamp on the back of the stem, undo the tensioning bolt, and it pulls off easily.

Fitting a stem is very simple: lightly grease the quill to stop any corrosion, put a dab of grease on the threads of the expander bolt and slide the stem into the fork.

How high or low you position the stem is up to you, but pay heed to the 'MAX HEIGHT' mark stamped on the side. If you want a higher position fit a higher stem; don't risk a shorter model on full extension. At the other extreme, some riders slide their stems fully down in the fork, causing the stem to bind on the headset. The weld on the underside of the stem will not sit properly with the headset and will undoubtably creak in use. Raise the stem so that the weld is 1/8inch clear of the headset locknut.

The expander bolt should be tightened so that the stem is tight, but not so tight that the bars won't turn in a crash. Holding the front wheel firmly between your knees, it should be possible to move the stem when pulling hard.

Aheadset users can simply push the stem onto the steerer, and clamp it in

Just a dab of grease is all that's needed to stop the stem being corroded

Loosening the expander bolt – if you're careful you don't have to protect it with a piece of wood. Notice that we've already slackened the front brake cable too.

place with the bolts. Ensure that the stem is straight when viewed from the top, in line with the front wheel.

Bar ends

Bar ends come in two types, 'cinch' models which clamp around the outside of the bar, or 'expander' type which use a wedge system to lock themselves inside the handlebar. Cinch types are light and fit any sort of bar, but take up some handlebar room. The expander variety weigh more, fit a certain number of bars, depending on their internal diameter, but don't take up any bar space.

Other differences between bar ends are in their shape and material. Short, slightly curved or L bend, made in aluminium, titanium or steel, all bar ends add to your climbing prowess.

Fitting bar ends

If your grips have removable end plugs, remove them. If not, tap the end of the bar to cut the end of the grip like a pastry cutter.

This will leave you with a grip with a hole in it. If you're fitting cinch bar ends, then the grips will need to be moved in by the width of the clamp of the bar end. Loosen and move the brake and shifter units inwards. Loosen the grips by pushing a thin screwdriver down between the grip and the bar, and squirting water in the gap. Now the bar end can be clamped or expanded in the correct position.

Don't turn the bolts hideously tight, but lock them up enough so that they don't move when you tug them. Comfortable positions vary, depending on your wants and likes, but between dead-flat and 30deg upwards is usual. Tighten the controls again, position brake levers at around 45deg, and shifters at about 30deg.

Don't tighten the stem bolt really solidly, or else when you crash the stem will not twist round. This may sound dangerous, but it's better for the component to slip rather than damaging you or your bike. It's easier to remove later

Tapping the ends of the grips with a hammer makes the rubber end bits cut a perfect circle. It's far easier than taking a Stanley knife to cut them down. Thank Onza not us for this handy hint

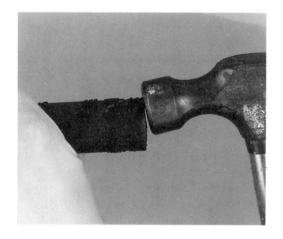

Like stems, bar ends shouldn't be tightened super-tight, just enough to stop them moving when you are pulling up on them. Over-tightening bar ends on lightweight bars can crush them

Setting up bars, stem and ends

Your bar and stem determine how your bike feels and handles. A longer stem puts more weight on the front wheel, changing the bike's handling characteristics. In extreme situations, too much weight on the front wheel can result in the front wheel knifing into the dirt and tucking under during cornering.

This can, however, also be the result of bad riding technique. Small frames shouldn't have long stems, but how long is too long? Take a plumb-line to measure the horizontal distance from the centre of the grips to the centre of the front axle. If the distance is less than four inches then the stem is too long, and more than six inches will mean that not enough weight is on the front of the bike. It will pop wheelies on climbs, just when you don't want it to.

The height of the stem is important for comfort and handling too. For several years I've been riding around on my bikes with the bars over five inches lower than the saddle. Dead racy and streamlined. My down-hilling was good, but after a back injury last year, I rationalised my riding position. Now my Pace has a 24deg stem which puts the bars 1.5 inches below my saddle. With 23.5 inch bars the difference is remark-able; I can now ride incredibly tricky downhills with new confidence, climbing is improved, and my back doesn't hurt either. Don't try to get a road position on your dirt bike.

14: SADDLES AND SEATPOSTS

Assembling and setting up the saddle and seatpost has ergonomic aspects as well as the mechanical issues we'd normally deal with. We'll attempt to cover the basics of saddle choice and adjustment, but there's no real substitute for experience and experimentation when it comes to your bike's set-up. The golden rule is to make small adjustments to one thing at a time.

Seatpost

As a mountain bike frame is smaller than a road bike's, a longer post is necessary to get the saddle height right. A greater length of tube sticking out of the frame means greater stress on this component. This, combined with the extra shocks from the lumps and bumps of off road riding, means that MTB seatposts have to be tough, and the old fashioned design – a pressed steel saddle clamp round a plain alloy seatpost – doesn't work for very long off road. Micro-adjusting posts with the clamp permanently attached to the post are stronger, and standard on most bikes.

MTB seatposts come in a huge range of diameters. In the old days when we all rode 531 framed road bikes, almost all seatposts were 27.2mm in diameter, but this size is found on only a few high-end steel MTBs, though it has become a *de facto* standard for a certain class of aluminium-framed bikes; both Trek and Cannondale use this size. For other MTBs the seatpost can be anything from 25.4mm to 32.6mm. This is a stock nightmare for shops. Take your old post with you when you go to buy a new one, and be prepared to wait for it to be specially ordered if its an unusual size.

Manufacturers claim all sorts of numbers for the length of their seat posts. For comparison purposes we use a measure called effective length, which is the distance between the maximum height line on the post and the saddle rails. Most posts have effective lengths of 260-350mm.

Posts are a significant area of potential weight saving. Standard posts tip the scales at around 300g; good lightweight ones are as light as 200g. We have seen some lightweight posts bend or break in use, however, heavy riders are advised to go on a diet or steer clear of very light seatposts.

Another way to reduce the weight of your seatpost is to trim it with a hacksaw or tube cutter. Mark the point on the post where the top of the seat lug comes, and measure the distance between this point and the maximum height mark. You can safely trim this much off the bottom

Saddle fixings

There are two main types of attachment systems to hold the saddle to the post, each with its advantages and disadvantages.

One-bolt design posts allow fine-tuning of the angle of the seat, because the cradle is usually grooved the angle adjustment is not infinitely fine. Even the best one-bolt posts can come loose under extreme conditions and should be checked regularly. The clamp of such a post usually has a small amount of rearward offset; almost all current frames are designed for a post like this.

To get the saddle off, you should be able to loosen the bolt until the top of the clamp can be rotated out of the way. Some posts have bulky clamps however, which will have to be removed completely. Re-assembling these posts is a bit fiddly; you have to hold everything together with one hand and screw in the bolt with the other.

The two-bolt clamp is usually more secure than a single bolt. These posts are incredibly susceptible to creaking, so it's best to grease all the parts, particularly where metal/metal contact occurs. Tighten securely.

Unfortunately most two-bolt designs put the clamp in line with the seat post (hence we sometimes refer to them as in-line posts). They therefore put you in a more forward position on the bike than intended by its designer, by one or two centimetres. If this is a positional change you need, then fine, but John finds it a

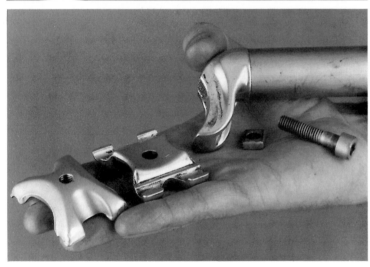

The conventional one-bolt design consists of an aluminium or steel clamp which bolts on to a curved cradle bonded on to an aluminium tube

of the post (see the advice on frame safety in Seatpost assembly first). Leave an extra centimetre for safety and don't let anyone with longer legs than you borrow your bike!

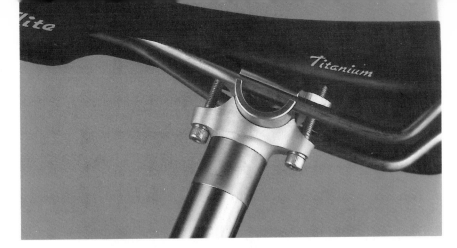

problem, and virtually everyone we've ever seen using one of these posts has been too far forward on the bike. The only two-bolt post with a standard clamp position is SunTour's excellent XC Pro, even if it is a little heavy by modern standards.

A double problem occurs if you use an ultra-long in-line post to make a bike fit that's too small, since the bike will almost certainly already be too short. Oddly, the riders we see most often with their bikes set up this badly are on incredibly expensive bikes. They'd be more comfortable on properly set up cheap machines.

Seat adjustment

Roadies have argued for years about the correct saddle height and position for most efficient pedalling. Whereas a road bike is set up to allow the rider to work most efficiently, a mountain bike has to take into account issues of traction and weight distribution that affect its handling off-road as well.

For general off-road riding the seat height should be set so that your knee has about a 15° bend when the pedal is at the bottom of the stroke. Downhillers might want to drop the seat a little from this standard to get it out of the way. You know your saddle is too high if your hips rock as you pedal. When you've got the height right, use a scribe to mark the top of the seat tube on the back of the post, so you can easily restore the correct set-up if someone borrows your bike.

Correct saddle angle is a matter of personal taste but it's worth experimenting if you're uncomfortable. Often, a small change can make a huge difference and it's a sight cheaper than buying a new seat. A good starting point is to lay a straight edge along the top of the saddle and adjust it so that the front and back are at the same level.

Many women prefer to point the nose of the saddle slightly downward to reduce pressure on the genital squishy bits (technical term). Don't overdo this, though – if the saddle points down too much you'll slip off the front, putting weight on to your arms and making yourself uncomfy. We have seen male racers with the saddle pointed slightly up. This plants you well back in the saddle for seated climbing and aids getting off the back for downhills.

The seat is also adjustable fore-and-aft, though most experienced riders just seem to slam it as far back on the rails as possible, with scant regard for roadie theories about how the point of your knee should be over the pedal spindle. A rearward position gives better rear-wheel traction, and this is a paramount consideration in setting up an MTB,

The two-bolt design, uses, er, two bolts, one at the front of the clamp and one at the back. By loosening one bolt and tightening the other the angle of the saddle can be infinitely finely adjusted, so this design offers true micro-adjustability

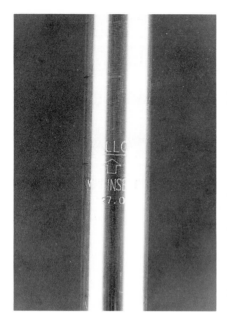

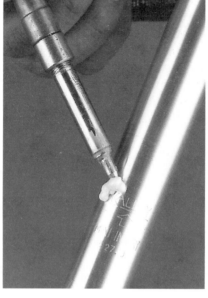

Find the mark on the seatpost which indicates the point which must be inside the frame — it will be marked maximum height or minimum insertion

It's essential to liberally grease the seat post. A clean aluminium post in a steel frame will corrode

much more so than tiny percentage improvements in pedalling efficiency. Moving the saddle forward makes it easier to spin the pedals at high revs, but unweights the back. Experiment for yourself and see what suits you.

Seatpost assembly

Make sure that the mark on the seatpost is inside the frame when the saddle is set at the right height. Alternatively, make sure that the bottom of the post extends to below the bottom of the top tube. This is particularly important for any frame which has an extended seat lug. We have seen frames broken at the seat cluster because the post doesn't extend far enough inside the seat

tube to support it. Seat tubes are designed to be supported by a close-fitting post right through the seat cluster area. If a post with an effective length of about 260–270mm isn't long enough you almost certainly need a bigger frame.

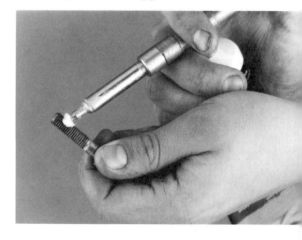

The steel saddle clamp bolt needs greasing for much the same reason that the post does. Leave it clean and the aluminium parts it screws into will corrode. It's important to regularly re-grease this area

Water, especially salt water, and the two metals set up a battery effect that turns the aluminium into aluminium oxide. This is bulkier than the original metal and the post therefore swells and seizes, often irremovably.

When you put the post into the frame, check the fit. It should slide in smoothly, with only the smallest amount of play, and the seat clamp should close about 0.3–0.7mm. A seat post that fits perfectly will slide gently down into the tube under its own weight when the seat post clamp is undone.

Don't lose the washer under the saddle clamp bolt. It allows you to get more torque on the bolt and, because it fits into the recess in the clamp, it's usually a hard-to-find size. If you're going to replace the bolt with a lightweight one, get a strong titanium bolt, made from 6Al/4V alloy not CP Grade II or aluminium.

If the post is the right size but the frame scratches it as it goes in, and there's a problem with the slot edges gouging the post, gently pry the slot open with a large screwdriver or carefully file away any burrs on the inside of the tube with a half-round file, making sure that the filings can't fall down the seat tube and into the bottom bracket.

Removing a seized post

If the post is corroded into the frame, the first thing to try (after kicking yourself for not greasing it properly) is to remove the seat bolt or quick release and spray lots of penetrating oil (WD-40, Duckoil) into the slot.

Take out the wheels, take the saddle off the clamp, and try and move the post by holding the top of the post in a vice and turning the frame. Don't go mad; too much brute force can wreck a lightweight frame.

If this doesn't work, a last-ditch technique is to take out the bottom bracket and pour caustic soda down the inside of the seat tube. Caustic soda dissolves aluminium but not steel, so it will get into the gap between the frame and the post and attack the post. Wear gloves and protective goggles while handling caustic soda. It's nasty stuff that cheerfully dissolves skin as well as aluminium, though it doesn't attack plastic.

If you do manage to get a corroded post out it will either need replacing, or, at the very least, careful sanding to get it to fit smoothly again. Use a fine-grade emery cloth and check the fit often.

Choosing a saddle

The comfort of the saddle, or lack of it, is the first thing a rookie mountain biker usually comments on. A comfy seat makes riding a pleasure, but an uncomfy one is enough to put most riders off cycling for good. Although most riders spend quite a bit of time out of the saddle, when you are sitting down the jarring from the trail far exceeds anything a roadie has to endure. It's therefore doubly important that a mountain bike saddle should be comfortable.

Oddly, comfortable doesn't necessarily mean bulky and deeply padded. Some riders find the new generation of minimalist, ultra-lightweight saddles very comfortable. What matters is that the hull of the seat under the padding should fit your particular shape well. If it doesn't, no amount of foam, gel or air bladders will make the seat comfy. The only solution is to get advice from other riders who are of similar weight and build to you, and ride a number of different saddles until you find one that fits you right.

There are huge numbers of saddles available: Specialized, Selle Italia, Selle San Marco, Selle Bassano (selle is Italian for saddle, in case you're wondering), Ritchey, Avocet, Velo and Vetta all make good ones, among others.

Women have particular problems finding good seats because, compared to a man, a woman has a wider pelvis and therefore wider spaced sit-bones, a shallower pubic arch and tender genitals. Female genitals are in exactly the right place to get squashed by the nose of the saddle and abraded by the motion of the legs. This is anything between uncomfortable and bloody excruciating. The answer is a wider, flatter saddle with less padding at the front. Specialized, Avocet and Vetta all make good saddles for women.

15: FRAMES

The frame of your bike is a remarkably lightweight structure considering the stresses that it has to cope with. The tubes are strong enough to allow you to plummet down hills or take big jumps in complete confidence, but they are susceptible to damage if they are dropped against a wall or in a big crash. Though the tubes on most mountain bikes are large in diameter, most steel frames have tube walls that go as thin as 0.6mm. That might make you nervous about riding hard, but don't be. They're plenty strong enough.

This chapter covers the areas you should check every few months, and also after a big crash, a huge set of jumps, and before making a mammoth cross-country trip. It's here where cleaning your frame makes sense; not by making it any stronger, but by allowing you to spot the start of any problems which could be catastrophic. Once much of the grime is removed from the frame, you can check the paintwork for any damage. No frame, whether steel or aluminium, will spontaneously develop a creased finish, or crackly paint for no reason. Crackly paint can be a sign that the tube underneath has moved, cracked or crumpled. As frames don't mend themselves, you need to look further.

Crash damage

Cars have a purpose built crumple-zone so that in the event of a crash they absorb the impact of a collision. Bikes don't. When you stack your bike, the frame, fork and wheels have to take the impact. The areas most susceptible to crash damage are the joints where the top and down tube join the head tube. If there's a strange creaking from the front of your aluminium bike, check here; there could be a crack forming.

Whilst steel frames have the attractive property of bending gradually, other materials aren't so handy. Titanium, carbon and aluminium frames all tend to snap rather than bending nicely. It always seems to happen at the point furthest from civilisation too. How do they know?

Whatever the frame material, with any sign of degradation stop riding immediately. In some cases, with some frames, it may be possible to replace the tube, but in a bad crash with a mass-produced frame it usually means a new frame is needed. Crash damage isn't usually covered by manufacturer's warranties, unless the damage has been caused because of a manufacturing defect − not usually the case. Don't complain when you don't get a free frame if you crashed your bike into a sheer-sided ditch.

Dented tubes

Dents in your frame are usually caused either by dropping the bike against a wall, or by the handlebars spinning around in a crash and denting the top tube halfway along its length. There's not a great deal you can do about them. If a dent is really big, and you're worried about it take it along to a reputable dealer or better still a framebuilder who will give you a professional opinion. A dent much deeper than a few millimetres is probably enough to affect frame strength, and could even have knocked the frame out of line. It all depends which tube it's in.

Chainstay damage

Though the top of your right-hand chainstay might look a heck of a mess from the chain bashing into it, it's rare for this to cause any structural damage. Most production frames have pretty thick walled tubes for their chainstays and though the outside may look battle scarred, deep down they're probably OK. Getting your framebuilder to fill any chainstay gouges with brass doesn't

Check these areas for frame damage, usually manifesting itself as crumpled or cracked paint

really make sense as the heat affected area of the tube would be weaker still.

There is a chance that with extreme 'chainsuck' the frame's integrity could be damaged. Chainsuck is the habit your chainset can develop, of keeping the chain on the rings when you change gear at the front, resulting in the chain dragging itself between the rings and the chainstay. It's weirder than corn circles, in that some people are plagued by the hideous phenomena, and others are never afflicted. Thin steel chainrings such as Onza's Buzzsaws or Pace's Extruder Groove system are recommended, and a clean well-lubricated drivetrain helps.

Front end collisions

In the old days it was much cheaper to have a crash on a bike. If you crashed you trashed a wheel. Crashed harder and you broke your forks. Now if you're running suspension forks on a production frame, a big front end crash won't touch the forks, but may result in the frame being snapped. It's a penalty for the better ride of suspension forks, but the extra control they give does mean that you crash less anyway.

Stacking a bike with rigid forks is much cheaper. If any damage is going to occur, the fork will usually bend backwards, and crease up. These big crashes are usually noticeable, because of the damage to the fork; several smaller crashes can cause worse problems.

Because of the use of curved forks on mountain bikes, it's hard to spot when collision damage occurs. You've just got to watch out for paint crumbling at the top of the blade. You don't have to be too clever to appreciate what will happen if your forks do snap.

Another possible problem that can happen with forks is the steerer tube bending. If the steerer tube bends, it will cause the headset to be tight when pointed forwards, but loose when positioned at 90deg. If you're unsure whether your steerer is bent, or it's simply the case of a loose headset, you can check with a straight edge when your forks are removed. Steerer tubes on steel forks don't tend to snap immediately, but aluminium models have been known to.

Suspension forks rarely get damaged in a front end collision, but it is possible to damage the crown or the stanchion tubes from an unbelievably heavy landing. Feel the back and front of the crown, where the blades are clamped to see if it has bulged out at all. Bent stanchion tubes will be apparent because of cracking chrome plate on the surface.

Frame alignment

If you've had a really bad crash, there is a possibility that your frame could have been knocked out of line. It could have been tweaked slightly across several joints so that there is

Check for fork blade alignment by looking from above and from the side

Headtube damage

Occasionally a badly machined headtube or one that's had downright hard riding can stretch. The signs will be the headset cups rocking in the frame, and the bottom (usually) edge of the headtube being stretched out. This is another repair that can only be carried out by a well-equipped shop or framebuilder, as the usual method of repair is to machine down the stretched section and then to reinstall the headset. In extreme cases a patch or reinforcing ring may have to be brazed onto the outside of the frame.

Scratch repair

Chromoly steel, by virtue of its chromium content, is reasonably rust-resistant, but it does need paint to protect it from the harsher aspects of the environment such as continuous damp and salted roads. It's rare for manufacturers to offer touch up paint with their bikes, and it's rarer still to find a colour that matches your bike down at the local discount motor store. Do not fear, as there is an easy way to keep your bike in tip-top condition and never get it scratched . . . don't ride it!

Scratches are a fact of life for mountain bikes, and users should be happy to let their bikes accumulate little nicks and knocks. For those really deep trailside scrapes it makes a degree of sense to touch them in. It's usually enough to touch in a scratch with paint, but you can go to

no paint cracking, no tube bending, but you could just feel that something isn't right. This 'funny steering feeling' will occur if the front wheels aren't following each other properly; the bike is out of track.

To check for frame alignment you need nothing more complex than a length of taut string. Wrap it from the rear dropouts, once around the headtube about half way up, and back to the dropouts. If your frame is in track, measuring from the string to the side of the seat-tube, the distance at both sides should be the same. If it isn't, the frame is out of track. 1-3mm is acceptable, but much more of this starts to play havoc with steering. Steel frames can be set by a good builder, but with other sorts, there's little you can do. Put up with it or scrap the frame. This is a good check to see the state of second hand bikes too.

the bother of rubbing down to the metal, touching in with primer and spray-fading to blend in.

Alternatively cover it with big stickers. This isn't as daft as it sounds; US manufacturer Bontrager Cycles have a huge vinyl sticker on their three main tubes, covering 3/4 of the tube area, protecting the frame. When they look battered, just replace a cheap sticker, rather than an expensive paint finish.

Repainting

After several years of use, your bike will look scruffy and tattered. You're then faced with either replacing the frame, or repainting and refurbishing your current one. Both options have their merits. A new frame will have more up-to-date geometry, though mountain bike geometry hasn't changed remarkably since 1990. Your old bike has memories for you, and you know its handling traits. It could be a question of being faithful to your past, rather than rushing into a new relationship with another frame, or it could be a question of expense.

If you get your frame repainted, you can have extra bits brazed on: bottle bosses, carrier mounts and bottle openers can all be added for a reasonable cost.

Framebuilders are used to dealing with steel frames, but aren't so familiar with aluminium, titanium or carbon models. If you have a frame in an alternative material, ask the painter if he's painted this material

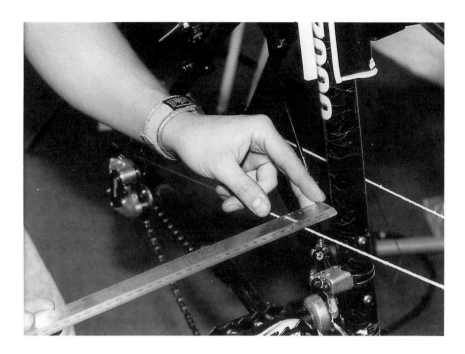

Measure the distance either side of the seat tube to the string. More than a few millimetres difference between each side means a bent frame

before. Bonded frames, or heat-treated frames don't like being cooked in an oven, the usual process of hardening bike paint.

As you'll have found, many manufacturers don't provide bikes with tough finishes, though of late it's getting better. Anybody wanting a tough finish would be best advised to seek out an electrostatic paint finish. Doggedly resilient to any knocks and nicks, epoxy powder coat is super-tough and will stay on your frame forever, only being removed by particularly nasty chemicals.

A sprayed enamel finish is tough too, and there are millions of possible colours and combinations available from many outlets. Whatever you do, don't take your bike along to the bloke who's more used to spraying Ford Cortinas. You're lightweight frame may well come back with a

Beyond repair . . .

whopping dent in it, which the guy will swear was there when you left it.

Bikes need special treatment when being painted, and they need cleaning up properly afterwards. Threads need to be retapped, the bottom bracket and headset need facing to accept the bearing cups again. Dealing through a reputable shop or established framebuilder should avoid any problems that could occur.

Don't be surprised to find yourself without your steed for a couple of weeks, at least. Frame painters usually have full order books, so don't decide to repaint at the height of the riding season when you want to be able to ride. Strip down times should be planned for yucky mid-winter.

16: OUT ON THE TRAIL

Many riders don't take any tools with them off-road, but trust to their bike's integrity and their own good luck. Others rely on their companions to bring along tool kits, as I did on a ride with several friends last summer. Crashing through bramble-infested tracks was a riot while it lasted, but eventually one of us got a puncture. Not to worry, we thought, as we helped Graeme replace his inner tube with the spare we'd brought. We'd just got Graeme's tube inflated with the CO_2 cartridges we were using, when another rider said 'Oh no, I've got a flat too!' Then, becoming wary, Graeme checked his front tyre and found he had another flat. Nearby was a field full of long, thick grass, so, recalling a tip we'd read in a magazine, we set about pulling bunches of grass from the field and stuffing tyres with them. No sooner had we got the two tyres stuffed than I got a flat too! Out with the grass again. The magazine said that grass stuffed tyres gave a good enough ride to get back to civilization. Cushy the ride wasn't, and having tyres that snaked around on the rims didn't encourage high speeds on the several miles of switchback downhills we had to ride.

One spare tube and two CO_2 cartridges between four riders isn't sensible. Unless you're riding through a latex plantation there's no way of mending a flat tube in the wilds, and even fewer ways of inflating it. So take plenty of spares. And here are a few tips for repairing your bike when everything around you seems desperate.

Trail tool kit

The best trail tool kit you have is your home workshop. For rides in the rough stuff, if your bike is set up correctly, you shouldn't have any problems. Bikes don't spontaneously fall apart; bits come loose or work incorrectly because they haven't been set up right in the first place. For this reason it's important to maintain your bike thoroughly all the time. Riders who take the 'only fix it when it's broken' approach are tempting fate every time they journey out on a ride. Some riders complain that they don't want to be weighed down by a bunch of tools jangling around under their saddle; but it's easier to carry two pounds of tools than to carry your bike home when it breaks.

As I said in Chapter 2, there's no need to take your full tool kit out on the trail with you. The basic trail kit listed on page 20 will usually keep you rolling along when the mechanical gremlins hit. Because you can't take your full tool kit with you, it's important to keep your bike in good condition. Every week or so, check the tightness of your crank bolts and headset locknut. If your freewheel or freehub is making funny noises, then replace or adjust it. These are all jobs that require big, heavy tools, sometimes even including a vice, that really aren't practical to carry even on the most extended trips. To that end, manufacturers have released more user-friendly products such as headsets that can be adjusted with only an Allen key, and bottom brackets that use pressed-in sealed cartridge bearings which rarely fail catastrophically.

Extended trail tool kit

Of course, if you're going to climb the Himalayas, you'll need more than a few spanners and some zip ties. The extended trail tool kit should consist of these extra items:

- **Headset and bottom-bracket spanners**
- **Crank puller**
- **6inch adjustable spanner**
- **Rear brake cable**
- **Rear gear cable**
- **Freewheel remover**
- **Two spare inner tubes**
- **Extra puncture repair kit**
- **Presta/Schrader valve adapter**
- **Schrader/Presta valve adapter**
- **Spare spokes**

A pair of headset and bottom-bracket spanners weighs about 1lb, less than a full bottle of water, but provided that your fixed cup is tight and well fixed in your bottom bracket, any adjustment needed can be done on the adjustable cup with a nail and a large rock. Ideal it's not, but it'll save you a lot of weight, and fitting an Allen key-adjustable headset and sealed cartridge bearing bottom bracket may be worth the money. The downside of cartridge bearing bottom brackets is that if the bearings pack up in deepest Tibet, you're going to be lucky to find a stockist of a 6003 neoprene-sealed bearing.

Tourists carrying lots of gear over heavy terrain can suffer from spoke breakages, though these are pretty rare unless the wheel is very old. Before going on an extended trip it's worth visiting a good wheelbuilder to have your wheels checked. If a spoke breaks, it is usually one of those on the freewheel side of the rear wheel, and is impossible to remove without first removing the freewheel. There are some 'get-you-home' spokes on the market, designed to hook into the hole without the freewheel having to be removed first. You can make up for a broken spoke by adding more tension to the spokes around it, but if several spokes have been broken, then the only thing to

do is to remove the freewheel and replace them.

You needn't take along a vice or a huge spanner, as if you're desperate you can usually get access to these, or just improvise. Someone with simple metalworking experience could make you up a piece of packing to allow you to use your headset spanner to remove your freewheel. US-based Pamir Engineering make super-small lightweight tools to remove Shimano freehub sprockets from their bodies. A crank puller, along with an adjustable spanner, will let you tighten or remove your crank arms, which is essential for bottom-bracket work or if you've got a particularly jammed chain. For extended trips in the back-country, take a spare rear brake and rear gear cable. A rear cable can always be used on the front, but not vice-versa. It's also practically guaranteed that every small village will have someone with a collection of large spanners and a vice. Barter, pay or beg them to help you mend your bike, and they probably will.

A three-inch gash in the sidewall of your tyre will render it useless, but thankfully one spin-off from the super-competitive world of mountain bike racing that benefits the tourist is the availability of folding tyres. Kevlar is used for the bead of racing tyres because it's much lighter than steel, but it allows the tyre to be folded up to about the size of a Coke can. If you really are going away from it all, a spare rear mech may get you out of having to ride home in one gear.

The further you're going, the greater the likelihood of punctures, so you should carry a couple more spare tubes and extra puncture patches. Valve adapters are useful, so that you can inflate any kind of tube using any pump you're likely to find.

Problems on the trail

Frame failures

You can carry spares to put on your frame, but carrying a spare frame would be considered pessimistic in the extreme. I once cracked a rear dropout at the start of a two-week touring holiday, so I walked into the local Tourist Information Centre and asked the assistant at the desk where I could find a welding kit! They were very helpful, and I found a garage who welded my dropout back together, allowing me to carry on riding. That was in 1987, and I've had several new bikes since then, but as far as I know that frame is still working fine today.

It's the question of reparability that is a big nail-in-the-coffin of many of the alternative materials on the market. Aluminium and bonded-steel framesets are coming into the mass market, where they usually offer a superb ride and low weight at a low price. However, for the expedition rider going miles from a cycle dealer, there's definitely an advantage in having a standard brazed-steel frame. In every town, be it in Nepal or Nigeria, someone will usually have a brazing torch and will be able to weld your bike back together if it cracks. That doesn't mean you can't tour on an aluminium bike, but if a problem develops, it's going to be hard to find a skilled TIG welder and heat-treating plant.

Broken rear mech

It's the most common problem, and also the most potentially disastrous for a mountain biker, when you've bent or broken your rear mech so that the chain won't run on the sprockets properly. Simply split the chain and rejoin it so that it doesn't run through the rear mech any more, reducing your twenty-one-speed to a one-speed in a few minutes. Put the chain on the sprocket that gives the best straight alignment with the chainring you want to use at the front. This will give you either a super-low gear with a small chainring and a large sprocket, a medium-paced gear with middle, or a downhill-all-the-way-home gear using the big ring.

Usually a bent rear mech means a bent gear hanger too. Check it, and if necessary fit a new one.

Of course, if you are going miles away from civilization, it's worth your while taking a spare rear mech. A cheap bottom-of-the-range model will cost you less, but will weigh more.

Crisped wheel

Sometimes you land so badly, or hit a ditch so deep, that you bend the wheel so hard it doesn't even turn in the frame. Chances are that you've damaged the rim beyond repair, so there's no point in pussyfooting about as you get the wheel sufficiently back into shape to let you ride it home. Take the wheel out of the frame, put it flat on the ground and hit it hard to force the rim roughly back where it should have been. Of course, if the wheel is only tweaked a bit, judicious use of your spoke key can get it spinning round again.

Bent forks

I've bent a few sets of forks in my time, and on every occasion have been able to ride home with them. If you pile your forks backwards, it may be that you can't ride because the front wheel is catching on the downtube, so you'll have to bend the blades forwards to give yourself enough room to turn the wheel. There's no 'correct' method for straightening bent forks, but it's best to pull on them hard rather than hitting them with something heavy. Replace them when you get home (see Chapter 14).

Ripped tyres

Sometimes you can rip the sidewall of a tyre when you puncture; then, when you reinflate the tyre, the inner tube will bulge out of the sidewall. If you ride like this for a while the inner tube will burst, but to prevent that happening you can put a patch on the inside of the tyre. Patches for mending punctures can be used, but a piece of paper or card works just as well, sometimes better. Pop the piece of card in between the tyre and the tube, install the inner tube, pop the tyre back on the rim, and reinflate. A spare lightweight folding tyre is compact to carry. It's a better solution than patching the tyre, and can save you a long walk home.

Chainrings

Sometimes you may hit a log or rock on the trail and bend a chainring, which may make pedalling impossible or throw the chain off when you try to use that ring. To straighten it, use an adjustable spanner to bend the ring back at the point where it's fixed to the spider. This should make the ring straight enough to ride home, though it's unlikely you'll be able to get it straight enough to allow it to run without chain-rub on the front mech. The ring will be fatigued, and should be replaced promptly. It's unusual to bend anything other than the big ring when hitting a rock, though inner chainrings can sometimes get very badly

mangled from chainsuck. If the worst comes to the worst, you usually have at least your middle ring to get home on. If your inner chainring is suffering from bad chainsuck, this is due to bent teeth or to scars on the side of the middle ring. If it's an alloy ring you can file the scars away with a rough rock, or even, as I did in one case, with the side of a matchbox.

Racks

If your bike's rack mounting bolts come loose and drop out, the Allen bolts that fit your bottle cages are probably the same thread, and can be used to replace them. If you haven't got enough bolts to go round, fit the ones you have in the dropout eye, and lash the top mounting point of the rack to the seatstays with heavy twine or a toe-strap. Racks sometimes break owing to the jarring they encounter off-road, but can be fixed with the help of a toestrap to lash the offending broken sections together; it's better to have a rack that works and no toestraps than not to be able to ride at all.

17: ANCILLARY EQUIPMENT

As you'll have found when buying extra bits of kit for yourself, your bike is only a part of the investment you've made in mountain biking. The shorts, shirts, waterproofs and boots that a year-round rider needs can easily add up to several hundred pounds' worth, so it's just as important to keep this equipment in good condition.

Waterproofs

The most popular breathable waterproof fabric by far is Goretex, a micro-cellular membrane sandwiched between two layers of material. W L Gore, who produce Goretex, used the technology from their artificial heart-valve work to develop the fabric.

Goretex works because the tiny perforations or pores in it let through water molecules in vapour form, but not the much bigger water droplets. It is just like the pores of your skin. Goretex must be kept clean to ensure that it works properly, though the newer grades are much less susceptible to clogging than the first-generation material. To keep the pores clear, your sweaty, mudded-up jacket should be rinsed in lukewarm water after every couple of rides. You can wash Goretex clothing in a washing machine, but make sure you only use Goretex detergent and wash at a very low temperature, otherwise you may affect the proofing or sealing of the garment.

Care must be taken when storing the material, too; the best idea is to hang it in a cool, dry cupboard. Folding it up and cramming it into the back of a drawer while it's still wet will quickly damage the fabric, causing the garment to leak.

Of course, waterproofs made from other materials can also be cleaned, but none of them should be washed at high temperatures. And never use detergent!

Other clothing

Sticking all your muddy clothing straight into the washing machine won't do your kit or your washing machine any good. In my garage I keep a large plastic dustbin which I fill with water after a particularly muddy ride to stick all my kit in overnight to get rid of the huge clumps of mud. Even after that, on the most intensive wash cycle, with the strongest biological washing powder, I can't shift all the mud stains from my white socks.

If the ride wasn't particularly muddy, do at least wash your shorts when you get back. Dirty shorts are a perfect breeding ground for the bacteria that cause saddle sores and other infections. It's best to hand wash shorts with soap (Lux flakes) rather than detergent. This helps to prolong the life of the fabrics and also prevents build-up of synthetic detergents that some people are sensitive to. If you find yourself getting odd rashes under your shorts try switching to a non-biological powder or soap. Lycra shorts should be dried on a flat surface away from direct sunlight as the UV in sunlight can degrade lycra.

Most cycle clothing, including jerseys made from polyester derived fabrics and fleeces, should be washed on a synthetics cycle. If, like many people, you use thermal underwear intended for mountaineering and like that as a bottom layer in the winter, don't tumble dry it; many of these fabrics melt at tumble-dryer temperatures. As a rule of thumb, avoid tumble-drying any cycle clothing.

Socks

Socks don't need any particular care, we just wanted to pass on some hard-won advice on winter footwear. When the weather turns cold and wet John and his wife Lesleigh still commute the 13km from home to office and have learned a lot about being comfortable. (Brant hibernates with a pile of videos and beer until March.)

Nothing will keep your feet completely dry. However, Bergaus Goretex socks over wool hiking socks will keep them fairly dry and they'll be warm even if they get wet. You may have to buy a second, larger pair of shoes, but believe us when we say it's worth it. A golden rule is that warm and wet is fine if warm and dry is impossible (ask any caver). When the weather warms up a bit then switch to Trek's wonderful wool ankle socks. These look just like normal short cycling socks, but they are lots warmer and are perfect for cool spring/autumn days.

Footwear

Don't chuck your mucky boots in the garage when you get home from a ride; they'll be rotting away until you dig them out for next time. Rinse them under the tap to remove the large lumps of mud, then stuff them with newspaper and let them dry slowly, not in front of a roaring fire. Every couple of months, check the condition of the laces. While it's not catastrophic, it would be annoying to have a perfectly functioning bike and then a lace breaks on you in the middle of nowhere. Hey, there's another thing to add to your tool kit — one spare shoelace.

Helmets

Even if you haven't had a big crash, you should always check your helmet for any dings or dents: big ones mean you should replace it. You should take care of your helmet, and store it where it isn't going to get damaged by something dropping on it. If you can remove the pads from the inside of your helmet, give them a wash every couple of weeks to stop any nasty bugs growing in them.

If you've had a crash and hit your head, then the helmet will probably have been weakened. Replace it rather than risk riding around with inadequate protection; you never know when you'll need it. Some manufacturers offer a free or cheap replacement policy for crashed helmets. Specialized will send you a new lid if you send them your trashed one, original sales receipt and a description of the accident; Giro will supply a new helmet for a nominal charge. If you're buying a new helmet, these are attractive options.

Waterbottles

Always rinse out your waterbottles after use. Drinking from a dirty waterbottle is a sure way to get a stomach upset. Bacteria love the damp close confines of the nozzle, and mould grows particularly well in the bottom of sticky waterbottles. If you leave your bottle with a few drops of energy drink in the bottom, when you come back to it the next weekend there'll most likely be a big lump of mould grinning at you through the top. While mould isn't generally harmful, it doesn't taste too great, so to get rid of it use a long bottle brush. If necessary, use boiling water with a couple of teaspoons of bicarbonate of soda to loosen the mould first. Rinse the bottle thoroughly with clean water, drain it and leave it to dry.

18: RECOMMENDED PARTS AND EQUIPMENT

The last couple of years have seen an explosion in the range and variety of mountain bike equipment, most of all in the field of lighter, stronger, or better replacement parts for the bits that come with your bike. It is now possible to take, say an XT-equipped bike and replace every single component except the derailleurs with a lighter, supposedly better, and usually much more expensive part. In some cases this is money well spent; in others, you'd be better off spending your cash on a week playing in the Pyrenees honing your bike riding skills.

Unless you enjoy spending money for its own sake (plenty of people do, and who are we to judge?) the best time to upgrade a part is when it has worn out or been damaged in a crash. You are then faced with a number of factors to help make a buying decision. If weight is a big issue for you, then you'll probably want to try and find a component that is lighter than the one you are replacing.

A useful measure of the comparative value for money of different lightweight parts is a number called the Hairsine ratio, which is weight divided by cost. It's named after expert class racer Jon Hairsine, who returned from a trip to France a few years ago with a lightweight carbon fibre handlebar which cost an unheard of sum of £40. He trimmed it to fit, and when asked how much he'd cut off, grumbled 'about five quid'.

Strength and reliability is another consideration. If you are very light and your riding style is very smooth, you can get away with lighter, less durable components. On the other hand if you are 13 stone of chaos and specialise in big air, downhilling, dual slalom and crashing . . . well, heavier riders need stronger, heavier equipment and should be buying on reputation for durability rather than weight. This usually means sticking with products from larger companies of the likes of Shimano, because these firms over-design to protect themselves from product liability problems. Quite simply the bigger firms are easy targets for hungry lawyers and so tend to make their stuff super-reliable.

Another issue is compatability. This is a particular problem with gear systems, but it does crop up in other areas as well. If you're replacing a component with a part from another manufacturer, find out if it works as well as the original; we'll deal with this problem case by case below.

Gears

Gear systems for ease and speed of shifting. Sticking with hyperglide used to mean using a complete set of mechs, shifters, hubs, chain and cassette. However, it is now possible to replace every component except the rear derailleur with a compatible part from another manufacturer. SRAM's Gripshift systems are a functional alternative to either thumbshifters or Shimano's Rapidfire Plus units; the latest chamfered Sedis chains shift as well as HG chains and are more reliable; lightweight hubs from Hope, White Industries and Ringlé, among others, will take Hyperglide sprockets and SRP's titanium HG sprockets work in place of Shimano's. All this is of course expensive.

SunTour's shift systems don't change quite so well as Shimano's, but have other advantages, not least of which is Micro Drive, a gear system which uses smaller sprockets and chainrings to improve shifting and save weight.

As far as personal recommendations go, John uses XT parts with thumbshifters on one of his bikes, and LX Rapidfire Plus on the other; Brant goes for XT. Generally, we get on well with Rapidfire but have a soft spot for thumbshifters, especially the alloy-bodied XT jobs. Neither of us use eight speed set-ups because of the additional rear wheel dish required, and neither of us have gone mad trying to make our bikes super light because we're not fit enough to justify the tiny performance difference a few titanium bolts make.

We've also steered clear of going to Shimano's eight speed XTR system because of the price, and because we feel that its superb quality of finish is actually overkill for mountain biking. It looks nice in the showroom, but that does you no good at all out in the mud.

As we write Shimano have just announced their line-up for the period mid-1993 to mid-1994. All their groups have switched to a Micro Drive style system that, for the mid-priced STX group at least, is actually heavier than the parts it replaces, because of the use of pressed steel chainrings, and has a poorer gear pattern (11/13/15/18/21/24/28 and 24/34/42 rather than the previous standard 12/14/16/18/21/24/28 and 24/36/46). The new sprocket cluster has some undesirably large gear jumps. In addition, the Rapidfire Plus shifters have acquired a little window that tells you what gear gear you're in, a distinctly underwhelming idea in the opinion of all mountain bikers who we've shown it to.

Brakes

In the face of stiff competition from the likes of Dia-Compe, Shimano revamped their brakes for 1993 and came up with M-system, a brake design that uses levers and calipers with high mechanical advantage, high quality cables and large, high friction pads to give the best braking the company has ever produced. Shimano brake weights are now down to about the same as Dia-Compe's. If you have a current Shimano equipped bike, there are few obvious reasons to change the brakes.

One reason, you may find, is if you don't like Rapidfire Plus. Since Shimano's shifters are mounted on the brake levers switching to Gripshift or thumbshifters means either grinding the shifter mounts off the levers or changing them. Many aftermarket levers do not work well with Shimano calipers. Levers with a fairly high mechanical advantage like Dia-Compe SS-7s and Ritchey logic work OK, though not as well as the originals.

It has been noted that M-system brake blocks wear out very quickly. Try replacing them with the new long-stud Aztecs. If you have a Dia-Compe or SunTour brake set you can improve their performance dramatically by ditching the stock blocks and fitting Aztecs. Do it straight away, rather than waiting for the old pads to wear out.

There are a few models of super light American made brakes on the market, but the performance gap between them and Shimano is now non existent.

Magura's Hydrostop hydraulic brakes and the disc brake systems from Mountain Cycles and Hope are the only real alternatives to cantilevers on the market at the moment. Hydrostops are great; with lots of power and virtually no maintenance they are Brant's first choice. We're told the Hope discs are very good, though neither of us has done much riding on them. The one Mountain Cycles disc we've used, which ran as the front brake on John and Lesleigh's tandem, worked brilliantly for a time, but needed its hydraulic system bleeding after every ride. This problem may have been cured, but, at the time of writing, there is no UK importer for these components.

Wheels

As we've said, we're reluctant to get into eight speed wheels because they are intrinsically weaker than seven speed, and we view the recent proliferation of eight speed systems with suspicion. These wheels are going to spend more time being trued and tweaked and not last as long as seven speed wheels. The reason is that the larger space needed for eight sprockets moves the drive-side hub flange over, creating a greater imbalance in the tension of the spokes. This imbalance tries to pull the wheel out of shape.

Wheel components need to be light and strong. We like Campagnolo and Bontrager rims, not least because it's easy to get tyres on and off them and Wheelsmith, DT and Ritchey double butted spokes. Double butted spokes actually make for a stronger wheel, while saving weight, for reasons to do with their flexibility. Aluminium nipples are another weight saving option, though Keith Bontrager recommends using them everywhere except the rear wheel drive side spokes, where stronger brass nipples are a better idea.

Lightweight quick release skewers are an easy way to save weight. We like those from Zero Components, Salsa, Ritchey and X-Lite. There are also some very good cheap Taiwanese skewers on the market, under a variety of trade names; look out for ones that have a nylon washer under the cam.

Pedals

Shimano's SPD pedal system is the dominant way for racers and hard-core riders to attach themselves to their bikes. It takes some time to get used to, but the benefits of not having to fiddle with clips and straps are well worth the effort. The cheaper LX version of the pedal works very well, and is actually simpler and less prone to clogging than the XT model. SunTour, Tioga and SR make excellent standard pedals (as do Shimano if you can find a set of standard XT pedals). Specialized make the best clips.

The success of SPD has led to other manufacturers wanting to get in on the act. Look's early off-road pedals, adapted from their road system, were hopeless, but their latest Nevada pedal which looks like a big SPD is pretty good, as long as you don't have sensitive knees. The Look system's complete lack of float could produce knee problems and can also get you into trouble when you need to move around on the bike. It's a bit too easy to come out unexpectedly. Time's Sierra and Extreme systems, on the other hand, have loads of float and are very comfortable and easy to move around on. Their main problem is that they are single-sided and therefore slower to get into than double-sided systems like Look and SPD.

We've seen very promising prototypes of Onza's system, which is the lightest of the four because it uses elastomer springs instead of steel, and has some lateral float built into the cleat.

At the moment both of us use SPDs.

Bars and stems

We both like our bars fairly wide, and are puzzled by the trend to 21.5inch bars that don't really leave room for bar ends. Our favourite bars are the Pace/Renthal RC-Sub 130 and Answer Hyperlite. Both are light but strong.

There are loads of good stems available; far too many to list. The one piece of advice we do give is that you shouldn't replace the handlebar clamp bolt with an aluminium one; they are not strong enough. We have seen at least one horrific accident as a result of an aluminium bar clamp bolt snapping at speed.

Saddles and seatposts

There has been a huge expansion in the range of saddles available in the last few years as seats have come under scrutiny from weight watchers and ergonomists. Sub-200g saddles are now commonplace (the good old Selle Italia Turbo, once the benchmark, weighs 320g) and seats in the 150g range like Selle San Marco's Concor Light are not unknown. The original Selle Italia Titanium Flite is a good choice for light, smooth rides but tends to sag under heavy loads. We also like Avocet's titanium-railed saddles, as well as seats from Vetta, Specialized and Bontrager. Where possible we suggest you try before you buy.

Women have a problem with saddles. (See Chapter 14) Being blokes we can make no recommendations from experience, but John's wife Lesleigh uses a Vetta Air women's saddle, and we have heard good reports of Specialized, Avocet and Madison women's saddles. It is our observation that any woman who gets into mountain biking in a big way is probably going to have to resign herself to spending money trying out different seats for a few months, because few saddle manufacturers seem to have much of a grip on this problem, and also because the problem is usually one of discomfort rather than excruciating pain. A suspension seatpost can help, and is a must if you are female and riding stoker on a tandem.

Seatposts need to be light and strong but they also need to put the seat in the right position. See Chapter 14 for more discussion of the issue of post clamp design and saddle position. We like the X-Lite ZE 360 post, SunTour's good old XC Pro two-bolt post and Specialized's light but inexpensive post. Syncros make the best in-line post.

Tyres

Racers increasingly choose tyres according to the conditions on the day, switching to lighter, narrower tyres when it's dry, using grippier fatter tyres for wet conditions, and fitting the very fattest tyres for downhill racing on rocky courses. For recreational use, when you're unlikely to change tyres from one month to the next we still like Ritchey Z-Max and Panaracer Smoke tyres, especially the lightweight WCS version of the Ritchey tyres.

Light tyres mean faster acceleration and a livelier feeling bike, but thin light tyres usually mean an increased risk of pinch punctures, less grip and a less comfortable ride because of the high pressure needed to keep a 1.9inch tyre away from the rim. In our opinion the trade-off is only worth it for racers.

TROUBLE SHOOTING GUIDE

Problem:	Reason:	Correction Required:
Chain no longer shifts smoothly from sprocket to sprocket.	1) Cables are dirty or stretched. 2) Chain is dirty or worn. 3) Rear mech or hanger is bent.	1) Clean and adjust the cables. 2) Clean and lubricate or replace the chain. 3) Straighten gear hanger and/or replace rear mech. See Chapter 5.
Chain doesn't shift smoothly from chainwheel to chainwheel.	1) Cables are dirty or stretched. 2) Chain is dirty or worn. 3) Chainwheels are loose or bent. 4) Front mech is bent or out of alignment.	1) Clean and adjust the cables. 2) Clean and lubricate or replace the chain. 3) Tighten chainwheel bolts, straighten or replace the chainrings. 4) Adjust front mech for alignment or replace. See Chapter 5 (Front Mech) or Chapter 7 (Chainrings).
Chain slips when pedalling hard.	1) Chain worn. 2) Sprockets or chainwheel worn (especially with a new chain). 3) Rear mech out of adjustment. 4) Freewheel mechanism worn or broken.	1) Replace the chain. Chapter 5 2) Replace sprockets and chainwheel. Chapter 7 and 8 3) Adjust rear mech. Chapter 5 4) Replace freewheel or freehub. Chapter 8
Brakes don't work effectively.	1) Brake cables are dirty or stretched. 2) Brake blocks are worn. 3) Rims or blocks are greasy. 4) Brakes out of adjustment.	1) Clean and adjust the cables. 2) Replace the brake blocks. 3) Clean rims and blocks. 4) Adjust the brakes to their correct position. See Chapter 6.
Brakes squeak.	1) Brakes are not 'toed in'. 2) Rims or blocks are dirty. 3) Brakes are loose on their pivots. 4) Some brakes always squeak!	1) Adjust the brakes so that the front edge of the pad hits the rim first. 2) Clean the rims and blocks. 3) Tighten the pivot bolts. 4) Buy new brakes, pads or earplugs. See Chapter 6.
The bikes doesn't steer 'properly'. It feels like it's wobbling.	1) Headset is loose. 2) Wheel cones are loose. 3) Stem out of line. 4) Frame cracked or bent.	1) Adjust the headset. Chapter 10 2) Adjust wheel cones. Chapter 8 3) Straighten the stem. Chapter 13 4) Examine the key frame breakage areas and consult a reputable dealer. Chapter 15
Pedalling is irregular.	1) Crank arm is loose. 2) Pedal bearings are loose. 3) Bottom bracket bearings are loose. 4) Crank, bottom bracket or pedal is bent.	1) Tighten the crank bolt. Chapter 7 2) Adjust the pedal bearings. Chapter 12 3) Adjust the bottom bracket bearings. Chapter 7 4) Replace the bent part. Chapter 7 or 12

FURTHER READING

It is impossible to cover all aspects of mountain bike maintenance in this book. There are several well-established, excellently written books available to help keen riders and mechanics take their skills further:

Barnett's Manual
Probably the most useful book around. It's incredibly detailed, and is like having a pro-team mechanic at your side 24 hours a day.

Sutherland's Handbook for Bicycle Mechanics
This is a suitable volume to accompany *Barnett's*. Containing comprehensive details of all aspects of bicycle components, it gives hints on how to mend parts, but it's most useful for information about a product. The wheelbuilding section covers most hubs and rims available, allowing you to calculate spoke length for any combination and any spoking pattern.

Bicycle Mechanics in Workshop and Competition
Steve Snowling, former team mechanic, takes you one step further in bike maintenance, and although aimed at roadies, his tips on team management may prove useful for those mechanics who really enjoy repairing bikes, and wish to work as a team mechanic.

Mountain Bike Magic How to Get the Most out of Your Mountain Bike
By Rob van der Plas, this book emphasises the charms of mountain biking. The excellent colour illustrations show in detail how to handle your bike under all conceivable circumstances. Technical information is restricted to that necessary for selecting components and keeping the bike in tune.

The Mountain Bike Book Choosing, Riding and Maintaining the Off-Road Bicycle
Another of Rob's books, this is a concise manual on the mountain bike and its use. The emphasis is on the technical aspects with clearly illustrated instructions.

Mountain Bike Racing
Simon Burney and Tim Gould are seasoned mountain bikers, and have put together this useful and informative introduction to the sport.

INDEX